Abuse

Questions and Answers for Counsellors and Therapists

By

MOIRA WALKER FBACP,
UKCP Registered Psychotherapist
Institute of Health and Community Studies
Bournemouth University

Series Editor
MICHAEL JACOBS

W
WHURR PUBLISHERS
LONDON AND PHILADELPHIA

© 2003 Whurr Publishers Ltd
First published 2003
by Whurr Publishers Ltd
19b Compton Terrace
London N1 2UN England and
325 Chestnut Street, Philadelphia PA 19106 USA

Reprinted 2003

British Library Cataloguing in Publication Data

A catalogue record for this book
is available from the British Library.

ISBN 1 86156 220 9

Typeset by Adrian McLaughlin, a@microguides.net
Printed and bound in the UK by Athenæum Press Ltd, Gateshead,
Tyne & Wear.

**Books are to be returned on or before
the last date below.**

Contents

Chapter 4   **67**

Therapeutic concerns

Chapter 5   **91**

The effects of abuse on the practitioner

Chapter 6   **115**

Service provision and supervision

Preface

In writing this book I have been continually aware of the number of people who have in some way contributed to it. They are too many to mention or to name individually, and the value and contribution of all is immeasurable. A particular group of people, and it is a large group, stand out. They are the survivors of abuse I have known in so many capacities over the years. They include very dear and significant friends, colleagues, students and, of course, clients. They are all remarkable in their capacity to have dealt so bravely with betrayal, pain and suffering and to have emerged as survivors and overcome victimhood. Their importance to me personally and professionally is immense and I hope this book in some way demonstrates how much I have learnt from them.

I have worked as a therapist with abuse survivors for many years now and have also trained others to undertake this work, and supervised many working in this painful area. I am continually impressed by the tenacity and bravery not only of survivors but also of those who care for them, and work with them. A particular mention must go to those who put such enormous energy into setting up voluntary services for survivors. I have been privileged to work with many of these as they struggle against many odds to set up projects and services that are literally life-savers for many, and they do it with few resources and often too little support. However, another feeling runs alongside. That is one of continuing horror at the scale of the problem; the forms it takes; the numbers involved; the appalling impact on the lives of so many adults as a result of childhood abuse, and the suffering and pain that is being inflicted, even as I write, on unimaginably large numbers of children.

Although this horror may be seen to be reflected in society at large it is yet to be translated into sufficient funding and sufficiently coherent and effective policies and service provision. If it is to have meaning it has to be backed up by money. And somehow we have to turn ourselves into a society that takes a wider responsibility for the well-being of children. They are our future and to ensure this they must be the responsibility of a larger community. Whilst services for the protection of children need to be scrutinized and need to be adequately resourced, the buck does not stop there. Children live in our streets, go to our schools, are our neighbours and part of our community. Turning a blind eye, seeing them as only the responsibility of designated others, is dangerous.

There is one person I do want to thank personally. That is my husband Michael Jacobs, the editor of this series and of this book. Although we have jointly edited books before this is the first occasion he has edited one of mine. We have not only equably survived the experience; he has as ever been a loving support throughout.

Finally, I should add that I hope this book adds, even if in some small way, to the understanding of the experience of abuse and assists those working with survivors.

Moira Walker
Bournemouth University
March 2003

CHAPTER 1

Initial issues and questions in counselling abuse survivors

1.1 How can abuse be defined? Is there any difference between the effects on the survivor of sexual, physical or emotional abuse?

Much is now written on sexual abuse, representing an enormous shift in thinking from the years when it was largely ignored, denied, or re-framed. Perhaps as a result of the concentration on sexual abuse less attention is paid to physical and emotional abuse, although the debate continues about whether or not physical punishment of children is acceptable. Many children suffer an appalling cocktail of all three forms of abuse. There are no neat dividing lines; for instance, sexual abuse inevitably contains aspects of physical abuse and emotional abuse. A child's body is invaded, and the tactics used by perpetrators to silence a child also attack the child's psychological well-being and sense of self. Emotional abuse can exist in isolation, although frequently it does not; whereas physical abuse is often accompanied by a verbally derogatory and destructive attack on the child.

Defining abuse is fraught with difficulty. Any definition is open to challenge, scrutiny or disagreement, and is inevitably time related and time limited. Child abuse is not specific to our present society, although the definition of certain behaviours as being abusive is. For example, physical child abuse could not have been defined as such until relatively recently. Kempe and Kempe, writing primarily on the physical abuse of children prior to the days when sexual abuse was becoming actively recognized, note that 'a book on child abuse could not have been written a hundred years ago. In the past it was largely invisible to families and their communities. Before it could be acknowledged as a social ill, changes had to occur in the sensibilities and outlook of our culture' (1978: 16). This is particularly pertinent to hitting children, which has a long history of being acceptable. The degree of violence and damage inflicted may be a question of debate, but the act of hitting itself has in many cultures been deemed

1

acceptable childcare practice, and it is part of a world in which violence, torture and uncontrolled aggression are sadly commonplace.

Physical abuse can be defined as physically harmful action that is intentionally taken against the child, usually resulting in visible injuries These can include bruises, burns, internal injuries, poisoning and broken limbs. However, some physical abuse is well planned, so that it does not leave obvious marks, or would do so only if the child was closely examined. Some children experience being bound and tied up for long periods of time, or hung upside down, often in the dark. Such treatment may not leave obvious signs of injury, especially when the abuser takes care not to leave visible marks. Comparisons to some forms of torture can be made here, where physical abuse can be carefully planned, and coldly put into action.

One stereotype of physical abuse is that it is either a justifiable slap from the parent, or that such a slap occasionally goes too far because the parent is stressed and loses their temper. This stereotype is often perpetuated by the critics of 'liberal' parenting, who continue to argue that smacking children is a positive force for good. Whilst that seems a deeply unacceptable method of child-rearing, doubtless that particular debate will continue to rage, doing the children who experience physical abuse a grave disservice, since it reduces and distorts their experiences. The 'smacking' debate distracts attention from a real issue, that each year children continue to be maimed, tortured and killed by parental violence.

Physical *neglect* should not be forgotten or minimized in terms of its damage and effects. Children can be deprived of food, clothing and of being kept clean, and their basic needs for warmth, care and nurture remain unmet. This is often perceived as more likely to occur in poor families but clinical experience suggests this is not the case. Professional and wealthy families can and do severely neglect children in these ways. They are, however, more skilled at hiding this neglect, and are therefore less likely to be detected.

One difficulty in defining sexual abuse is whether this involves only actual contact, or whether non-contact events should be included. Another is the age of the perpetrator: a current concern relates to older children abusing younger children – but what age gap is necessary before one child can be deemed to have abused another? Can a 10-year-old child, for example, abuse another of the same age? Or would this be harmless 'playing' or 'experimentation'? (see Question 2.6).

The following is my own broad working definition of sexual abuse:

> It is essential to recognise as crucial elements the misuse of power and authority, combined with force or coercion, which leads to the exploitation of children in situations where adults, or children sufficiently older than the victim to have greater strength and power, seek sexual gratification through those who are developmentally immature and where, as a result, consent from the

victim is a non-concept. Such gratification can involve explicit sexual acts –
anal or vaginal intercourse; fondling; masturbation, or may involve invasive
and inappropriate actions not directly involving contact: watching a child
undress, bathe, use the toilet, in order to gratify the perpetrator rather than
meeting the needs of the child; forcing them to watch adults having sex or
making them watch pornographic videos. What is central is the exploitation
of the child; the denial of their rights and feelings; and the essential gratification of the abuser through the child, the child being regarded solely as an
object for the perpetrator's use and to meet their needs. (Walker, 1997: 59)

Emotional neglect and cruelty can take many forms. It can be horribly fla-
grant as in the killing or torturing of children's pets or the threat to do so;
intentionally frightening a child with tales of monsters, and then waking
them at night pretending to be one. More subtly, but potentially equally
harmful, is continually putting a child down: telling them they are stupid;
suggesting they are crazy or imagining things; scapegoating one particular
child in a family; ignoring or rejecting them; by placing impossible
demands upon the child that cannot possibly be met. The last may be literal demands – for example, asking a 3-year-old to take good care of their
6-month-old sibling whilst mother goes out; or a psychological demand –
for example, to make and keep mother happy.

De Zulueta (1993) defines emotional abuse as a 'form of child maltreatment which can take the form of consistent negative attention such as
repeated criticisms or belittlements, or a lack of attention such as with-
drawal or rejection'. One example of emotional abuse is a young man, who
was constantly belittled by his father as a child and young person. Father
continually watched him, gave him no space to play or even to be, and sys-
tematically criticized everything he did, although this was always
accompanied by expressions of concern for him ('This is because I care
about you; you have to learn' – the sadist's mantra). According to his father
nothing associated with the son was any good: anything he achieved was
flawed, and he came to believe that he himself was essentially useless and
invalid. His mother was depressed (not surprisingly as she seemed to be
similarly treated), and did nothing to intervene.

Trying to compare the effects of different types of abuse is as complex
as attempting a set of definitions. This is partly because, as noted already,
abuse is often a nasty cocktail of different behaviours. Additionally, so
many variables are at work, some of which are discussed in the answers to
other questions: for example, the age of the child when abused; the relationship of the abuser to the child; the gender of the child; the duration of
the abuse; whether any effective interventions occurred; other support in
the child's life. These factors complicate the picture. In my clinical experience of working with adult survivors, all forms of child abuse can have the
most enormous and serious impact on the child and the adult; but the

factors already referred to, along with other issues, play their part in determining how much and what sort of damage is done. (Walker, 1992). The following observations of the different effects of abuse need to be understood within such a context.

Survivors of any form of abuse can be deeply confused about the nature of loving relationships. Survivors of physical abuse can find distinguishing love from violence particularly problematic, and survivors of sexual abuse often have difficulty in distinguishing love from sex. Although all forms of abuse cause relationship problems, it seems that sexual abuse is particularly likely to lead to later sexual difficulties. This can also arise with survivors of physical abuse, but it seems less common, and in my experience more easily accessible to therapeutic intervention.

Emotional abuse, as described powerfully by Vas Dias (2000), has profound effects on the individual. Emotionally abusive parents offer the converse of what their child needs. Instead of attunement and appropriate space there is lack of empathy, often accompanied by a bizarre combination of abandonment and invasion. Instead of the baby 'feeling grand' (Kohut, 1977), the child experiences herself as a useless impediment; and the encouragement to discover and be oneself is replaced by a consistent demolition of that self. Vas Dias describes the 'inner silence' that results (2000: 160). In my experience this dismantling of the person is intrinsic to emotional abuse, leading to a sense of non-being, as if there is a shell of the person with little inner, sustaining, substance. This is in some respects a powerful contrast to the experience of some sexual abuse survivors. Whereas the emotionally abused child lacks any sense of being special, the sexually abused child can feel, in a horribly distorted way, all too special, and this has potent consequences for adulthood. Compare the experience of the young man in the example above with that of a young woman who was groomed by her father for abuse from an early age. She was emotionally separated from her mother, being her father's 'little princess'; a child 'with magic powers' over her father. She was, as he groomed her, made to feel she was unique, the only one able to meet her father's needs. As a young woman beginning to unravel and understand the effects of her father's abuse of her, one feature apparent in working with her was her grandiosity and narcissism. She experienced herself as all important in her current world; everything resulted from her special power. This could seem almost psychotic in nature, and yet in terms of her history it made entire sense. Therapeutic work with both these young people was long term and complex. In each of them their sense of self was grossly distorted and disturbed by their abuse, and yet manifested itself in vastly different presentations.

For the abused child, the unpredictability of the abuse is terrifying: it can come at any time and in any place, although certain scenarios and settings carry special risks. Generally life becomes uncertain, insecure and untrustworthy. Some survivors of physical abuse recount a different experience, involving a horrible predictability. One woman described difficulty in knowing whether to call her experiences abusive, or whether she had simply been the recipient, along with her siblings, of a very strict disciplinarian father who believed in physical punishment. Today the treatment she described would be clearly labelled abusive, but the dilemma in her own understanding of her experience relates to the debate about definitions of abuse that are culturally and historically bound. What was significant for her was that the ill-treatment was entirely predictable. There were clear rules and if they were broken there was a violent response; if they were kept there was not. As an adult she experienced considerable difficulties as a result of this treatment, but she did not feel that danger lay around every corner. She felt that her 'bad' behaviour had been attacked rather than the core of her self. This is in direct contrast to another woman, who had experienced quite unpredictable violent attacks from her severely mentally ill mother. She recalled that even as a child she recognized that mother's assaults had more to do with mother than with her. Because of her instability, this mother had been incapable of creating the clever falsifications and justifications used by many abusers, whereby blame and guilt are projected on to, and then introjected by the child victim. Both the women clients I describe here had been able as children to make some external sense of what was happening to them, and this appeared to minimize, although not prevent entirely, the internal, psychic damage caused.

In my own work with survivors it seems that the effective repression of memories (see Question 3.3) has a particularly strong association with sexual abuse. Survivors of emotional and physical abuse usually have a clearer and more easily accessible recall of events. Survivors who have experienced more than one form of abuse are more likely to have 'lost' clear memories of sexual abuse, whilst being able to recall and speak about other painful experiences. Instances of sexual abuse are also more likely to be replayed through flashbacks and spontaneous regression than is apparent with either physical or emotional abuse. Additionally, sexual abuse survivors seem particularly prone to a deep uncertainty about their perceptions of their world. As children, the reality of their abuse was so effectively denied, simplified or distorted by the perpetrators (for example, 'You like it'; 'You made me do it'; 'It's our special little game'), that as adults they find it difficult to accurately recognize or trust their own judgement.

The differences described here indicate only certain key areas that may be apparent. What is essential, when so much attention is given to sexual abuse, is to recognize the equally profound effects of physical and emotional abuse.

* * *

1.2 Does the age of the child at the time of the abuse make a difference? Or whether abuse is perpetrated by a mother or a father, a relative or a stranger, of the same or the opposite sex?

For every child the significance of their primary relationship to parents or parental figures is both central and wide-reaching for their well-being and their satisfactory development. Any disruption to it has significant and major consequences. The existence of a safe attachment and a secure base (Bowlby, 1988) is essential. Children learn who they are and what sort of person they are through their earliest relationships. These boundaries of the self are established both physically and psychologically, and these two aspects are interwoven. Their establishment arises from the early communication and relatedness between baby and child and their significant others. Stern (1985) describes the 'dance' of baby/parent interaction, helping the child to begin the process of knowing, recognizing and valuing herself. For the child who is abused by a parent this attachment and identification of self is complex: the person they need and trust for protection is also the one the child needs protection from. Hurt children cling to their caregiver, but when that person is the perpetrator, the child is caught in a psychological and developmental trap.

The particular age when a child is abused interrupts this developmental process in different ways, but it is inevitable that if the abuser is a close caregiver, and the child is very young, the damage is likely to be considerable and long-lasting. Anyone who has ever seen the frozen watchfulness of a young child or baby who has been physically abused will recognize the horribly damaging consequences. Although research evidence on the significance of the age of the abused child in relation to later impact of the abuse is mixed (Meiselman, 1978; Langmade, 1988), clinical evidence suggests that the younger and more dependent the child the greater the damage, particularly when the abusers are parents or primary carers. This is because of the developmental needs of the young child.

For example, a woman in her twenties had suffered sexual abuse from her stepfather from the age of 12 to 14. Her father had died when she was 10. She had enjoyed a very close and loving relationship with him and a good relationship with her mother. The advent of stepfather changed the family dynamics radically, and he was also violent to mother. However, by this stage this child had acquired a very strong and positive sense of self. She had good internalized objects and clear memories of loving and nurturing care from both parents. She never doubted that stepfather was in the wrong; she did not hold herself responsible, and at the age of 14 was able to tell a trusted teacher. As a result, she was then moved to live with her grandparents. Her losses were considerable and the damage great, but her presentation of self, her perceptions of self and her basic trust had been dented but not destroyed. This was essentially different to how another survivor presented, with a similar history but occurring earlier in her life. It is particularly problematic for a young abused child to find a way of integrating her experiences or of making sense of them. My clinical experience leads me to think that very early, very severe abuse is highly likely to become split off, so that dissociative disorders can result.

Children who are abused by either parent can effectively lose both parents: one through the abuse and the other by psychological default. For example, if a daughter is abused by her father or stepfather this breaks into the mother–daughter bond. It drives a wedge between them, and is preventable only if mother is told and acts both to stop the abuse and to support her daughter (Burstow, 1992). For a more detailed discussion on why a mother is often not told see Walker (1992). In this scenario the abused child becomes a psychological orphan: father is abusing her and mother is not protecting her. She feels betrayed by both. Both mother and daughter are humiliated and subordinated by the abuse, and the power of the abuser smashes the mother–daughter attachment. Research certainly suggests that abuse by father or stepfather causes greater trauma than that by other abusers (Finkelhor, 1979; Russell, 1986). Similarly, a child who is abused by her mother when father does not intervene loses both parents. She is left without any safe attachment; her parents as 'good enough' objects have been destroyed. This dynamic is of course further intensified if both parents are involved in the abuse, and even more so if the parents are implicated in an abuse ring. Clinically the effects of abuse are most severe when both parents have been involved.

Another crucial stage for the child (Erikson, 1965) is the development of physical and psychological autonomy. This is especially complex and problematic if both genders have abused the child, since the child feels her or his body is completely owned by others.

Research into the effects of abuse by women is limited. Most studies suggest that men constitute about 90 per cent of perpetrators, although others (e.g. Mendel, 1995) dispute this, arguing that female abuse is much higher, but that it is denied, wrongly construed by the studies, or simply not reported. Two studies that explore the sex of the abuser in relation to its impact find that male sexual abuse is more traumatic (Finkelhor, 1979; Russell, 1986). This is in direct contrast to my own clinical experience, which indicates that female abuse is especially traumatic and viewed as a very particular betrayal. The research may itself be limited by the difficulty of survivors and others in acknowledging female abuse, particularly where it is sexual. It remains problematic to accept that women can and do abuse, especially when it is their own children. Both male and female victims share a particular concern that they will not be believed if they were sexually abused by a woman. The idea contravenes the stereotype of the loving, nurturing mother and woman, particularly in a society where so much of childcare is entrusted to women. Abuse is inevitably perceived and experienced via a cultural filter and, given the emphasis on women as safe carers, awareness of female abuse of children may be distorted. The picture is further complicated in that abuse often involves more than one person, and the same child can be abused by both men and women. In my clinical experience it has frequently been reported by survivors that they have been physically and/or emotionally abused by mother and sexually abused by father or another close male relative. As children who are abused within the family are also more prone to victimization and abuse by others (Finkelhor, 1979), unravelling the various strands in terms of the differential effects of gender is complex.

In terms of stranger abuse, or abuse by a more distant relative, it has to be recognized that this too can create the psychological orphaning of a child. If the child is unable to tell, or is not believed when they do, then the parent–child attachment is seriously weakened or even broken. The child has no safe figure to run to and to trust, and effectively becomes abandoned in her pain, distress and terror. Many 'stranger' abusers are in fact not strangers. They may be unrelated but still be close and trusted figures: neighbours, teachers, babysitters and close family friends. Research is contradictory on whether the closer the relationship (that is, within the family) the more traumatic the abuse. This may suggest that other variables are as significant: the degree of trust the child has placed in the abuser; the significance of the abuser in their lives; the quality of other relationships; the level of betrayal experienced; the amount of fear induced in the child, and the nature of the threats that substantiate this fear.

An example of enormous damage from abuse outside the family is of a man abused by the son of his teacher for four years from the age of 6. The teacher was a very close family friend. The son was entrusted with babysitting, and the families used to go on holiday together. They lived nearby. As a child this person felt there was no escape. His own parents were experiencing financial difficulties, and his mother had been ill. There were very clear messages that the children had to be good – this was a precarious family emotionally. The abuse was bizarre in nature, and accompanied by sophisticated threats. The abuser was seen every day by the child. The child's whole world and his total safety came under consistent and ongoing attack. For two years the abuser's father taught him, while at home the victim's family constantly praised the abuser and his father for their friendship and support. It was a crazy world for this child as friendship, education and abuse were horribly intertwined. As an adult he was dissociated, unable to form relationships, self-harming and at times seriously suicidal.

This is a very different scenario clinically from that of abuse by an unknown person, itself a much less common presentation: the greatest risk to a child remains from within their own familiar world. A woman in her twenties recalled how she had been sexually abused as a little girl of 8. She had been grabbed in the park when playing alone, after an argument with the two friends she was supposed to be with. It was a serious assault, but she had been rescued by a passing woman who heard her scream. She took her back to her parents. The police were involved, and therapeutic help was given to her and her family. Her parents, grandparents and older sister, although very distressed, were supportive and loving: she described being 'wrapped in a blanket of love'. The assault was talked about, and she was actively encouraged to say how she felt and to express her feelings. For a year after the assault she described herself as 'regressed and clingy' but she was allowed to be like that, and then gently encouraged back into the world. Although in her twenties she was left with some residual anxieties, particularly in terms of sexual relationships, she was nevertheless very accessible to further therapeutic help. Her basic trust had not been destroyed, as it had been for the man in the previous example. She consciously and clearly recognized the source of her difficulties and was very able to work with them. She had good supportive relationships within and without her family, and it was clear that the damage had been limited by the availability and resilience of her primary attachment figures.

There is another aspect to this question that relates to the long-term effects on boys and girls of abuse respectively by women and by men. A study by Petrovich and Templer (1984) found that 59 per cent of rapists in their study had been sexually abused by women in childhood. Mendel (1995) also argues that sexual victimization of boys by women is a particular risk factor for later sexual assaults on women. Some researchers (Finch, 1967; Finkelhor, 1984b) have found a link between the sexual abuse of boys by older men and later homosexual behaviour. However, others (Bolton et al., 1989) have pointed out that 'the roads to a homosexual orientation are many', and information to date does not provide sufficient clarity to identify which cases might resolve themselves in such a manner (Bolton and Bolton, 1987).

Clinically it appears that a particular confusion and conflict can be created by same gender abuse. Mondimore notes that 'abuse by a male perpetrator appears to cause male victims to question their masculinity and their sexual orientation in profound ways' (2000: 151). Abuse by the same gender perpetrator can lead to the male and female victims wondering if this will determine their sexual orientation; it can create anxieties that maybe they look like the opposite gender, and that it was this that triggered the abuse. It appears especially hard for a girl to achieve a separate personal and sexual identity if she has been sexually abused by her mother, and this creates considerable difficulties around the area of motherhood. For both girls and boys, same gender abuse can result in a difficulty in the differentiation of self. A key developmental task of early childhood is to differentiate one's own body from those of the parent or carer. Sexual abuse by the same gender parent can blur this essential distinction.

* * *

1.3 What are the clearest indications in presenting problems in adults that abuse might have taken place in childhood? And how can I help someone to disclose?

As I note in Question 3.1 on eating disorders and substance abuse, it is always dangerous to assume that because a certain symptom is present therefore abuse is the likely underlying issue. It remains true that there is a strong link between such behaviours and abuse, and this is also true of self-harm, but there are dangers in simply providing a checklist whereby a client presenting with particular symptoms becomes significantly likely to have been abused. However, it is helpful to possess a map that provides an idea of the range of the territory, as long as this does not lead to automatic assumptions: assumptions and a checklist mentality have contributed to survivors being forced down particular treatment routes and labelled unhelpfully or inappropriately. It should also be recognized that any map is incomplete and always has to be redrawn in the light of new knowledge. What we know is not absolute but is fluid and developing. However, on this basis it is possible to identify aspects of presenting problems that may be related to abuse. This answer provides an outline of some of these.

Abused children have had the boundaries of their self and their bodies invaded, and adult clients can present with serious boundary difficulties: they may as yet have no way of saying no. This may be reflected in a pattern of unsatisfactory and sometimes abusive relationships, often accompanied by a history of sexual difficulties or dissatisfaction. There can be a real confusion between love and sex and pain, both in receiving and giving care, love and sex. Child abuse devastates the sense of self-worth, and adult survivors often have very poor self-esteem, accompanied by feelings of not deserving anything good. This has enormous impact on all relationships and can lead to the destruction of various aspects of life (e.g. jobs, relationships) that are potentially or actually positive. Some survivors experience a powerful attraction to negativity: there is a real and profound difficulty in allowing anything good to happen. The good is both wanted, but rejected; desired but feared. This outlook can be accompanied by a deep sense of alienation and isolation, and difficulty in trusting anyone, carrying with it implications for all relationships, including those with a counsellor. Although the client may not say so specifically, they feel that closeness is dangerous (as it was in their abusive childhood experiences); and this is a particular aspect of their difficulty in trusting. It is not only relationships with partners that are problematic; it can extend to all others, including those with friends and even their own children.

Anger and rage are commonly experienced by abuse survivors, and this can be acted out against others in violent behaviour, destruction of property (e.g. arson) or other crimes, or can be turned against the self, such as through self-harm or by destroying the possibility of good things. Acting out is a reflection of an inability to communicate distress verbally: abused children have little or no experience of being encouraged to do so and the adult may still be unable to. Conversely, anger may be acutely feared, accompanied by inappropriate over-compliance and anxiety to please. As well as fearing anger, there can be a deeply embedded but generalized non-specific fear of the world as a dangerous place. The adult client, although unclear as to where danger lies, nevertheless feels surrounded by it, as indeed does the abused child. There can be an enormous anxiety about confidentiality that links both to the difficulty in trusting and experiencing the world as inherently unsafe.

Depression, sometimes accompanied by suicidal feelings, anxiety and panic attacks, is common in abuse survivors, and can often appear unrelated to obvious recent causes or triggers. Although a contentious area – discussed in more depth in Question 5.7 – memory can be affected by abuse, so survivors often have gaps in their memories, particularly of childhood years. Consequently there can be a fusion in the line between reality and non-reality. Problems in sleeping are often reported: survivors may be hyper-vigilant at night-time, particularly if as children they were wakened from sleep to be abused. Sleep may also be disturbed by nightmares, and some survivors actively try not to sleep because the nightmares are so real, invasive and disturbing. The content of the nightmares is frequently violent and catastrophic. Day-time flashbacks (see Question 3.5) are also frequently experienced, although clients may have difficulty in talking about these, believing that flashbacks indicate madness or mental disturbance. This is particularly so if they have had poor experiences in the psychiatric system. Other perceptual difficulties can be present: for example, feeling an evil presence is inside them; hearing children crying; hearing non-existent noises or experiencing actual but innocent noises as deeply threatening; believing shadows to be persons or monsters. In terms of the child experiencing severe abuse these false perceptions make entire sense, but again the survivor may fear the label of mental illness, and often has reason for doing so.

Many survivors complain of feeling dirty and have to continuously wash themselves and their clothes, and obsessively clean their homes. They also report high levels of physical illness: severe headaches, stomach ailments, skin disorders, back and throat pains are common. In addition, there is a high level of mental ill health and admission to psychiatric hospitals. Sadly, they have often experienced abuse in the care system, either directly or by organizational structures: for example, by perpetrators and victims being in close proximity with no way of avoiding or protesting against this; by wrong diagnosis and consequent wrong treatment; by lack of knowledge leading to inappropriate or unhelpful or damaging responses and labelling. This can lead to survivors appearing deeply suspicious when they turn to counselling or therapy for help: they may hope for a different experience, but their previous encounters with the caring professions make them suspect it will be the same.

Many survivors are initially very reluctant to talk about their abuse, so it is important to be aware of these indications that it may have taken place, whilst at the same time taking care not to suggest it, and to pace any interventions around the subject. At the same time the client needs permission to tell their story; so what helps and what hinders survivors in disclosing?

Direct questioning about possible abusive experiences needs to be used cautiously: it may occasionally help, but needs very careful timing, together with sufficient degree of certainty that it is appropriate. Direct questioning can be experienced as invasive (the client feels obliged to answer even if they would prefer not to), creating a feeling of being trapped. If direct questioning is used during an assessment this may precipitate a crisis for the client, who then may need immediate help, but might be faced with a long wait for ongoing appointments. The client may not be ready to disclose; or is unsure if they have been abused; or is sure but feels able to say this only within the context of a trusting relationship. A client faced by a direct question who chooses not to answer, evades it, or answers untruthfully, can later fear being accused of lying, so repeating earlier patterns and experiences.

On the other hand, a survivor client told me that during a long stay in psychiatric hospital no one had ever asked her what she thought was the problem. If they had, she would have told them of the abuse. However, she made it clear she wanted to be asked what was troubling her, rather than have specific suggestions made to her. In many years of working with survivors I have found that most have experienced very direct questioning, whether in a questionnaire or face to face, as unhelpful, worrying and invasive. Few have found it useful. When it has been helpful it has been as the result of knowing their counsellor, who has been listening attentively to their struggle to tell their story, and who empathically responds with a direct question at a point where the client needs help in order to speak. This is totally opposite to the checklist questioning many have experienced, which has borne no relation to their needs but is part of a set intake procedure.

Disclosure can also be hampered by previously unhelpful experiences of trying to speak. It is useful to check out with a new client about any previous helping experiences. Some clients find themselves with the 'wrong' counsellor: for example, if they have had no choice regarding the gender of the counsellor. The sense that a counsellor does not want to hear, or cannot cope with or contain such information, will quickly be recognized and adversely responded to by a client. An over-emotional response from a counsellor who appears very angry, shocked or distressed will also constrain the survivor in speaking, just as will conversely lack of response from a counsellor who is too distant or is perceived as being uninterested or disbelieving. Other unhelpful factors are the client feeling rushed, or feeling there is an expectation to tell; if the boundaries of the session are not held and the client does not feel safe; and if there are anxieties about repercussions of disclosing or concerns about confidentiality.

What helps a client disclose is a safe, pleasant and confidential environment, where there are clear boundaries set out and held by the counsellor. For instance, some clients have a trial run by saying a little just before the session is due to end. In this way they limit both how much they say and the therapist's response. It can be deeply threatening when this strategy (which may be unconscious) is not recognized by the counsellor, who then extends the session and does not allow the client to control the time for themselves. A better response is for the counsellor to acknowledge that he or she has heard; to note that it may be difficult to talk about; and to reassure that there will be plenty of time in the weeks to come to say more, if and when the client wishes. This acknowledges what is being said, holds the boundaries and respects the client. The therapist makes it clear that there is no pressure to say anything, but that he or she is prepared to hear anything when the client is ready. The counsellor needs to be sensitive to signs that a client wants to disclose, and to provide a calm, warm response that communicates care and belief, and the counsellor's ability to cope with such disclosure.

If disclosure is made on assessment, or when the client is going to be referred, he or she may need help not to say too much – without suggesting that the therapist does not want to hear. This needs explaining to the client. It helps also to acknowledge that disclosure is a major step, and to invite the client to look at her or his feelings, having disclosed, without labelling or naming them, as they can be different for different people. Time needs to be allowed for the client to explore these feelings, as well as to consider how he or she will cope before seeing the therapist next time, particularly if this is the first time of telling anyone. The client may also need reassurance that abuse of children is serious, that it has serious consequences into adulthood, and that this may contradict what he or she had been told as a child.

It needs to be remembered that disclosure is a process not an event. It is not a neat recall or summary. It may be fragmented, come in fits and starts, and may not always make sense; or it may be like freeing a 'log jam', so that once the client starts disclosing it may be hard to stop (in the same way as the abuse could not be controlled once it began). Disclosure starts a process of working with the material, and can create dilemmas and difficulties for the client: once the information is out it cannot be disclaimed.

Client anxieties that may need to be addressed can include: anxiety that talking about the abuse may make it unbearably real again; that they cannot be exactly sure it happened; fear of what will happen if they tell and how they might react (for example, might it trigger self-harm or a suicide attempt?); fear of the abuser's threats being carried out (remembering that the child victim is often silenced by threats of death or damage to their families, their friends, themselves or their pets); that their current life is already difficult and that disclosure will make it worse; worries that if disclosure begins what else may emerge; that the disclosed memories might induce feelings of badness, guilt, shame and horror; and fears about judgement or blame from the counsellor, even if this is unspoken.

Yet disclosure can also provide a sense of relief that a secret that once seemed impossible to speak of has now been shared, and that there is hope of resolution. In the context of a sensitive and trustworthy relationship that recognizes the pain and anxieties inherent in the process, disclosure sets the scene for the work that needs to be done, and for the healing journey that is ahead.

* * *

1.4 Are there particular areas I need to consider and to be aware of when beginning to work with an abused client?

The ways new clients experience the start of counselling varies. Seeking help is always a big decision to take and some will feel relief and a sense of accomplishment, especially if it has been a struggle to make this move and find help. Others have had previous experiences that may or may not have been helpful and, if the latter, they will be cautious and anxious in case the therapist is yet another unhelpful person. So for some, it is a first attempt to relate their story, whilst others have tried previously. Whatever else, they are likely to be anxious, uncertain and watchful, and will be cautious in respect of the counsellor, looking for signs as to their trustworthiness.

It is worth noting that survivors of abuse may be seen in a specialist service for abuse survivors, in which case they will already have identified themselves as such, but many are seen in generic services. In this situation the counsellor may or may not know in early sessions if abuse is an issue, but may wonder about an abusive history. This presents an early dilemma, of wanting to ensure the client feels enabled to disclose if they wish (see Question 1.3 on disclosure), whilst avoiding being suggestive (see Question 5.7 on 'false' memory). If the counsellor is not careful there is a further potential therapeutic trap of being perceived by the client as abusive, by pushing them into facing and saying things before they are ready; or as someone who denies or colludes with abuse by apparently refusing to see or hear what the underlying issue may be. This is a delicate balancing act to achieve, where the counsellor demonstrates a willingness to hear everything, without the client feeling they have to say anything.

Some clients have come entirely of their own free will, while others have been persuaded or even pressurized into coming. This has implications for the client's response to counselling even before they have set eyes on their counsellor. Others have been referred by the person from whom they initially sought help. They can have strong feelings about this, either negative or positive, but equally significant for the client who may feel rejected, anxious, or even strangely satisfied that they have somehow been 'too much' for the previous helper. Many will minimize their difficulties and experiences; abuse survivors have a very low self-image anyway, and making light of difficulties represents an attempt genuinely to make them more manageable. Facing the enormity of abuse is very painful, and simply being seen by someone can feel threatening. So from the first they may be ambivalent; both wanting to see the therapist and talk; but *not* wanting to see or talk to the therapist. Coming to a counsellor is an acknowledgement that help is needed: it can be a massive step to take, even if for the counsellor a new client is an everyday occurrence.

It is important to be aware of the potential significance to the client of the organization of any agency where counsellors and therapists work. It is worth carefully considering if it is user-friendly and welcoming; if it is aware of issues of oppression; if it is aware of client/counsellor power issues and whether it gives the client a choice of counsellor in respect of gender and culture. For counsellors who have become used to their own agency, it is sometimes hard to remember how intimidating it can be: for example, finding the way in; not knowing where to park your car, or how to get there from the bus stop. Waiting areas need to be pleasant and private. Reception areas should not be part of a busy thoroughfare where others are busily chatting, socializing or passing messages to one another. These are important for any client in any agency, but have particular concerns for the client who carries issues of abuse.

In the early stages the counsellor needs to offer and clarify confidentiality. If there are agency limits to confidentiality, the client needs to be aware of them from the start. This is again important in any counselling relationship but has special significance for abused clients. They must not experience counselling as abusive, and failure to maintain confidentiality, or to be honest about its limitations, is an abuse of trust. For those treated previously in other agencies or institutions where confidentiality has been less seriously or honestly considered, this is a particular issue.

It is essential that the relationship between client and counsellor develops on the basis that the client feels they are taken seriously and believed. Central to this is careful, empathic and attentive listening, which really attempts to understand what the client is saying from their point of view.

It is important to be aware of the misuse of power in the adult's own childhood and to take the greatest of care not to misuse power in the counselling situation. For example, it is important to make it clear that although the client had no control over what happened to them as a child, they can control the pace and development of counselling sessions. Assurance needs to be given that the client may proceed in their own time; that they will not be pushed into revealing detail that they are not ready to talk about or cope with, but that when they are ready to disclose more, the counsellor will listen, will not be shocked or overwhelmed, and will support their client. At the same time, awareness of boundary issues is vital, remembering that all abused children have had their boundaries invaded. The therapist needs to clarify the boundaries of time, place, length of counselling (both for each session and in terms of ongoing duration, whether it is time-limited or open-ended), and contact out of sessions, and should never offer more than he or she can realistically give.

It can be difficult for an abused client to have to sit away from the door, or not to have the door in view. They may need to have their back to a wall, and may be particularly disturbed by interruptions in the session, which of course should not happen in the time allocated to them. Change of room or time over which the client has no control can also be difficult. All counsellors need to be sensitive to these issues and take them seriously, and if sessions are interrupted, or venues or times unavoidably changed this should not be ignored, but acknowledged, taken seriously and worked with.

Particularly during early stages of the work, it is not helpful to allow prolonged silences, since these can be very threatening to the client. A relational style is more appropriate, one that acknowledges the difficulties and anxieties that the client may be experiencing, and helps the client begin to express them. It is neither surprising nor inappropriate that abused clients find it difficult to speak freely, especially initially, and it is important to validate that difficulty. I have already indicated in Question

1.3 the threatening nature of questions; formal history-taking can also be invasive, so that explaining why information helps the process may make it less difficult for the client.

* * *

1.5 As counselling progresses are there particular dynamics or therapeutic issues that I should be especially aware of?

Part of the answer to this question is discussed in the questions about trust (1.6) and about the counsellor's own feelings (5.2). I also refer in Question 1.4 to the importance in the beginning of the work for boundaries to be put carefully but clearly in place. As the work continues these may be challenged by the client, who has herself a history of boundaries being constantly under attack. It is crucial that these are maintained firmly, that they are effective as part of the containing of the client, and that the boundaries do not strangle the work: the counsellor has to take responsibility for this. This should not of course be done in a punitive or aggressive way.

The dynamics of abuse can be powerfully repeated as the counselling process progresses and this has constantly to be borne in mind. It is obviously necessary to be gently supportive and containing, but there is a dilemma in being so. The counsellor who is attempting to help the client pace the work, and to deal with their experiences in manageable portions, may be perceived as ineffective, uncaring or uninterested, or of being well intentioned but doing nothing, like those who colluded or ignored in childhood. However, if the pace of the work is not carefully monitored the client can feel disempowered, out of control, and once again invaded. What is important, although not always easy, is to help a client to recognize a theme without forcing them into looking at it. They must always be given a way out in their response, as they can easily feel trapped into responding, just as they were trapped in their experience of the abuse.

The counsellor can sometimes experience anxiety as to whether to say certain things or not; he or she feels damned if they do and damned if they don't. They may be caught in a situation where any response feels extreme, even though what the counsellor wants to convey is not intended that way. As with abuse itself, it can feel difficult to move, with the middle ground being hard to locate. As noted in Question 1.4, silence can be very threatening, but conversely saying too much can be overwhelming, with the client feeling as flooded by words as they were overwhelmed by the abuse. The danger is that the counsellor feels so paralysed that they really do become unable to intervene, thereby becoming as powerless as the abused child.

Another dynamic relates to pacing and control, where a client may want to say no to the counsellor, but experience of abuse has given little chance of saying this in the past to anyone seen as a powerful person. So there can be discordance between the counsellor and the client. The counsellor believes that they have carefully and genuinely stressed that the client has an absolute right not to explore areas she is not comfortable with and to say no to the counsellor if she wishes. The client hears this, agrees and understands at one level, but at another is quite unable to act on intellectual understanding because emotionally she reacts submissively. So the good intentions of the counsellor may be quite ineffective, without addressing the client's lack of experience with assertiveness, or her deep belief that it simply leads to worse abuse. This can be further reinforced by the survivor feeling, often unconsciously, that she needs to be compliant and pleasant in order to avoid further abuse.

Counsellors need to be able to tolerate not knowing, not always being able to make things clear, and not always being able to help. They also need to help clients tolerate not knowing and lack of clarity. For many survivors, abuse is a shadowy affair, difficult to define and describe clearly, particularly if it took place when the child was very young. Although for some the picture is clearer, or becomes clearer as the work progresses, and some are able to have their experiences verified or clarified by others, many are left facing uncertainty, areas of confusion and gaps in their lives. This does not mean they are not able to recover and move on, but it does mean helping them to acknowledge incompleteness and lack of certainty in their past. To do so, the counsellor must also feel comfortable with uncertainty. Counsellors who need always to find clear answers, or to be definitive, are not going to help the many survivors whose lives do not match such a simplistic outlook.

* * *

1.6 A new client, who was referred to me as someone who was badly abused as a child, is finding it difficult to talk to me, although she knows she wants to speak about the abuse. It is all very tense and painful. How can I help her to trust me?

Trust is in many ways the cornerstone of personal development, central to enabling any good and nurturing relationship to take place: 'Basic trust is the developmental achievement of earlier life' (Herman, 1992). For the abused child, the destruction of trust is central to their experience. Their trust in the abuser has in itself been open to exploitation as he or she used it to gain their own ends. Perpetrators of abuse consciously and intentionally manipulate the trust of a child, and Salter notes how 'some offenders rely exclusively on trust and rarely even discuss secrecy with the child'. She continues by quoting an offender: 'Well, first of all I've won their trust. They think I'm the greatest thing that ever lived because I'm so nice to them' (Salter, 1995: 88). A study by Warner-Kearney (1987) shows that 90 per cent of fathers who had committed incest deliberately worked at building trust with the children they intended to abuse.

In this way, trust becomes the key to abuse rather than the key to a good and respectful relationship. It is also highly significant that many abusers are those deemed by society to be trustworthy: parents, relatives, carers, and church ministers, to name but a few. Similarly, counsellors and therapists are deemed to be trustworthy and ethical, but for abuse survivors the question of why a therapist should be any different may be unsaid or even unformulated; but is nevertheless powerfully present in the interactions with the counsellor. Counsellors have to prove their integrity and earn trust. This question suggests the client was referred by someone else, so there may be an issue for this client in terms of her readiness for counselling: was she really in agreement with the referral? was she unable to say no? had she perhaps hoped to see the person who had referred her? is she pleasing someone else? It is always worth checking the level of reluctance in the client, remembering that abuse survivors have little experience of being safely assertive and saying no, and that any attempts to do so have often been entirely disregarded.

Since trauma destroys trust, rebuilding this within a therapeutic relationship cannot be straightforward. If it is achieved it can enable the client to move forward, not only in dealing with past abuse, but by facilitating the development of trust in other current relationships. This rebuilding cannot and will not be smooth: it is a process and not an event, and a process that in itself moves through various stages. It will be tried and tested many times over, sometimes challenging the ability of the practitioner to stay constant throughout. Survivors may miss sessions, come late, sometimes choose to talk, and sometimes feel unable to. Timing is of the essence. Difficulty in speaking needs to be acknowledged. Clients also need to know that it is perfectly acceptable to offer snippets of memories and feelings. Experiences cannot always be clearly recalled and cogently expressed: there may be no words to describe them anyway. It often feels a mess with a mass of confusing images and pieces that do not as yet fit. Not only does the client need to know they can reveal this mess; they also need to know that the counsellor can calmly contain it without prematurely trying to impose unreal order upon it.

When abuse survivors have had their boundaries invaded, those they expected to be most reliable have proved themselves to be the most unreliable. So it is important for the counsellor to be reliable, to be on time, always to give as much notice as possible of planned breaks, and to deal sensitively with unplanned events, such as illness. The creation and maintenance of clear and safe boundaries of time, place and behaviour are essential. For the client to be believed and affirmed and to know that what they say is confidential are also basic features to the process. (See also Question 1.4, on the importance of clarity in relation to agency policy on confidentiality.)

Counsellors must be resilient and robust themselves, as clients need to know that what they say, and how they present themselves, will not cause damage, will not overwhelm nor frighten the counsellor. They need to know that the counsellor can cope and that it is not the responsibility of the client to care for them. Practical factors matter too: giving a client the choice of where to sit, with permission to move the chair if they need to (see also Question 1.4). For some, even being in a room with a closed door is too frightening and too reminiscent of their abuse. Yet an open door conflicts with the need for confidentiality and privacy, and the privacy of other clients in a busy building. If the setting does not allow for open doors, the fear can be acknowledged and the client invited to check that the door will open, and invited to sit near it.

Careful, empathic listening with well-timed and paced interventions, aids the development of trust. Similarly, it is crucial to understand and be sensitive to the ambivalence a survivor may feel towards receiving help: it is both desperately wanted and needed, and yet also feared. In understanding the difficulty of building up trust it is important to remember that for most children and adults closeness is a positive and nurturing experience, but for abused children and adults closeness is dangerous: it means invasion and lack of autonomy and power. It means being made to feel ashamed and made to feel humiliated.

The point at which trust is beginning to develop is a dangerous time for the survivor. A vivid example of this is given by Salter as she describes the view of a foster mother: 'When a sexually abused adolescent tried to get too close to her she quietly set limits on it. "Because I know", she said, "That's when they run. When they get too close to you. They can't tolerate it and next thing you know they've run"' (1995: 183). Although this example relates to younger clients, and such a response may not be quite so sharply defined and transparent with someone older, nevertheless the same dynamic operates. It is crucial that practitioners create a safe space in which interventions are not overwhelming in their content, length or style, and where silences are not too long and do not become frightening and oppressive. Similarly, the creation of closeness and intimacy has to be understood as a dangerous area (see Question 1.5). It is also worth noting that for some abused clients who place trust in their counsellors and therapists, this proves to be yet another abusive and exploitative relationship (Rutter, 1990). Research shows that it is women clients with a history of childhood abuse who are most likely to be re-abused in a therapeutic situation. This serves to highlight the need for counsellors to take the utmost care to hold extremely carefully to appropriate boundaries.

* * *

1.7 How will I know when to end the counselling with a survivor?

This question obviously does not arise for counsellors and agencies who work within specified time limits, whether short-term or longer. The ending date is set at the beginning, held in focus throughout the process, and actively acknowledged with the client in the context of deciding with them what can reasonably be worked on and achieved within that time span. However, if the work is open-ended the question becomes particularly pertinent. The negotiation with the client that takes place in focused work should still be present in open-ended work, and there too the ending should be kept in mind: the work will not go on forever and both clients and counsellors need some sense of what is hoped to be achieved by the time the counselling concludes.

Bearing in mind that any checklist must take into account the individual nature of the difficulties a survivor experiences, the following considerations may be useful in deciding an appropriate point of ending:

- Does the survivor have a more positive self-image, and is he or she able to pursue and choose what they want, whether this is education, relationships or careers?
- Is there evidence of an improved self-liking and self-esteem, and of the ability to enter and maintain positive relationships, in which the survivor can allow appropriate dependency of others on herself or himself, and of self on others?
- Is there more understanding of the impact of the abuse, and how it may repeat itself in the present (this is often discovered through the relationship with the counsellor), but now with more ability to recognize, manage and contain this?
- Has the survivor grieved childhood losses and been able to move on and allow good things to happen? Is he or she able to take their place in the world and feel they have a right to be there?

- Is there a better ability to tolerate difficult feelings, to recognize, acknowledge and overcome present-day difficulties, and to know that difficulties need not become disasters?
- Can the survivor allow personal mistakes and mistakes by others and in relationships, without seeing these either as betrayal or as devastating, but part of life?
- Is depression managed satisfactorily and is it within tolerable limits?
- Is the survivor able to meet her own needs and express her own feelings?

It is important for counsellor and client together to recognize that the aim of counselling is not perfect resolution or absolute cure. Life is not like that for anyone. New memories may surface after the ending; some difficulties will still be present, and painful feelings will have to be coped with. The client needs the tools with which to cope, but they do not need to seek perfection – it does not exist. Through the counselling relationship the survivor can learn transferable skills to deal with the wider world. It is also important to stress that if at any point in the future the survivor needs more counselling this does not represent a failure; rather it demonstrates the survivor's growing self-awareness and self-belief, if they are able to identify difficulties and seek appropriate help. Palatable portions of therapy and counselling can be helpful and appropriate: in this way therapy can be used as a 'top-up', when new issues are faced, or when old ones take on a new significance, for example when a survivor enters a new relationship or becomes a parent.

Chapter 2

Concerns of survivors

2.1 I have a client who is convinced he is going to abuse children he meets through his work, because he was abused himself by a vicar when he was a child. He says that it is a well-known fact that survivors of abuse go on to abuse others. Is he right to be so concerned?

Perhaps the most infamous consequence of abuse of the child is when the victim grows up to abuse their own child, or other children – what is known as 'the cycle of abuse' (Steele and Pollock, 1968; Oliver and Taylor, 1971; Groth and Burgess, 1979; Hunter and Kilstrom, 1979). Although apparently well documented, researching the cycle of abuse carries obvious methodological difficulties (Egeland, 1988): many adults who were abused as children were never identified and are therefore not visible as a distinct and recognizable group for research purposes; many adult survivors who are parents have never come to the attention of child protection or other relevant agencies and consequently are similarly invisible; and research into high risk parents and their children (Egeland et al., 1987) clearly focuses on a particular group. Other studies criticize an over-simplistic causal link between childhood abuse and adults who become perpetrators (Herman, 1988; Hooper, 1995).

There is always a danger of falling into extreme and falsely dichotomized positions on abuse, and the cycle of abuse question exemplifies this. On the one hand survivors groups understandably resent the suggestion that victims become victimizers: it is unfair labelling, derogatory, and potentially piles further loss on to other losses – many survivors are scared of having children of their own in case they too abuse (Walker, 1999). It is equally unhelpful, however, to define victims and perpetrators as completely separate groups that never overlap. Clinicians know this false divide does not apply; and in working with victims and survivors it is crucial to recognize and be aware that some will also be abusers, and that others may be at risk of offending against children. This recognition can be problematic for the practitioner.

Although it is known that some male perpetrators of abuse were themselves victims as children it is not possible to estimate accurately the numbers of those who were abused yet do not offend. Clinical experience suggests that many abuse survivors do not become perpetrators; and indeed many clinicians know a large number in the general population who have been abused and who become neither clients nor perpetrators. As in other areas, knowledge is woefully incomplete and any assumptions are dangerous. Russell (1984) suggests that male victims who go on to become perpetrators are different as a group from those who do not, but that identifying what distinguishes these two groups remains problematic and uncertain. An open mind is essential and it is evident that some clients who present for counselling or therapy, both men and women (but particularly men), express fears of becoming like their perpetrator. For some, this is simply based on the mythology of the cycle of abuse: they see this as inevitable and unavoidable – a direct consequence of their own abuse. However, others do have reason to be concerned, and a therapist or counsellor working in this field must be prepared for the latter, and not fall simplistically into reassurance that there is nothing to worry about. Where there is concern, practitioners need to be able to work with this either themselves or through referral to an agency or individual with specialist knowledge and skills in this area. It is argued that 'there seems to be room for clinical alertness in situations involving previously victimized male children. Staying open to the possibilities is not equal to an assumption that deviant sexual behaviour will follow every abuse of the male child's sexuality' (Bolton et al., 1989: 3).

A client's concern therefore needs to be taken seriously. As far as this particular example is concerned it is not possible to know if this client is right to be so concerned. It is crucial to acknowledge the anxieties and begin to unravel their origin. Is this simply a case of an abused man who has become terrified by hearing simplistic but powerfully told stories that link child abuse to future offending? Was the trigger for the expression of these worries at this point in therapy an immediate and panic-stricken response to such external factors? Or is this someone who experiences sexual urges towards children, or who has fantasies of harming them and who only now feels safe enough to express them? The question of why such fear is expressed now is therefore crucial. Finkelhor's model (1984a) of the preconditions of sexual abuse can be helpful in assisting the clinician to assess the risk of potential child abuse, but like all models should be treated with caution especially by those with little experience in this field. Finkelhor's preconditions are grouped into four categories:

- motivation – does he find children erotic and sexually desirable?
- internal inhibitions – is he able to overcome the internal inhibitors that would militate against abuse?
- external inhibitions – will he be able to overcome external obstacles and inhibiting factors?
- resistance – will he overcome the child's resistance to sexual abuse?

Essentially, therefore, the client must be allowed to raise these worries, without false reassurance or making premature assumptions. The counsellor or therapist, within the context of a good and sound therapeutic relationship in which an effective working alliance has been formed, needs to help the client address their concerns. If there is sufficient evidence that the client's concerns have a real basis then several factors need to be considered. The first is to consider what type of help is going to be most effective. The second is to recognize any limitations of the counsellor's skills and expertise and the possibility of the need for referral. The third is to remember that counsellors and therapists work within a legal and ethical framework, and need to check that their decisions take this into account. Consulting a knowledgeable supervisor, and if necessary drawing on specialist supervision and expertise, is essential in these situations. It is also important to recognize that if a client is expressing fears of abusing, this can be a crucial time for effective therapeutic intervention that ultimately may reduce the risk to children.

It is also important to be aware that paedophiles are skilled at insinuating themselves into jobs where they have legitimate and socially approved access to children; and this may be the case with the client in question. If there is real concern that in an attempt to deal with his own abuse the client will act out on others, it is not sufficient to assume that the therapy currently being offered will be able to deal with this. It may or it may not be; and this needs to be explored honestly with the client with the possibility of locating further skilled help. A client who is honest enough and trusting enough to express such worries deserves a similarly respectful response. Whilst this dialogue and exploration is in progress it is very important that the quality of the therapeutic relationship is maintained, and again supervision can help with this. It is extremely anxiety-provoking for the counsellor to be party to such concerns, and then to turn them into unhelpful countertransferential responses in which he or she retreats from the client and the therapeutic process. Remember that it is possible to continue working with a client whilst they are receiving specific assessment elsewhere. It may thereafter be possible to continue therapeutic work as long as it is 'contained' elsewhere under the umbrella of a specialized service that supports, supervises and assesses the specific concern. This may be anathema to those who would see this as interfering with the transference, or disturbing the purity of a process, but therapeutic flexibility and creativity may be essential when such difficult and complex scenarios are encountered.

The question posed here raises difficult issues, but another possibility exists for the counsellor attempting to unravel the meaning of this client's fears. In working with survivors of abuse, practitioners need to be aware that there may be an unconscious desire on the part of the client, expressed transferentially, to make the counsellor suffer as he or she suffered, to frighten as he or she was frightened, and to destroy the therapeutic relationship that is simultaneously desired and enormously feared. The threat that the victim may turn perpetrator is effective in creating a frightened and suffering counsellor. Similarly, the counsellor who refers on too precipitously, without sufficient exploration and preparation, or withdraws emotionally, fulfils the client's fears and becomes yet another person who cannot cope or who rejects. All too often this repeats a childhood pattern of adults who did not want to know or did not respond helpfully to hearing what had happened.

These points are made in the context of counsellors and therapists being used to the client being the key person in the process, with the therapist's responsibility being clearly to that person. However, this is challenged when we work with clients where there is a central concern over the protection of children (Briggs, 1998: 110). This is not to argue against working with perpetrators – and those who work with survivors will sometimes find themselves in that position – but it has to be recognized that the needs and rights of the adult as a perpetrator has to take second place to the safety of children. This is a difficult judgement to make and decision to take, but it is one that cannot be avoided unless we are to collude with the denial that perpetuates child abuse.

* * *

2.2 I have a client, herself abused as a child, who is a very anxious mother – anxious lest her own daughter is abused by her partner, even though rationally she knows this is very unlikely. How can I help her to trust him?

The decision to have a child is a major one. For some women survivors there can be an overwhelming desire for a child, and particular significance can be ascribed to that child thereafter. A baby provides hope and the potential for restoring normal family life that many fear their abuse has destroyed. Children inevitably serve a multitude of functions in the family and can act out unconscious desires/needs of the parents, including their internal conflicts; children can occupy a crucial psychodynamic role in the family. But there are complexities: the child is longed for, but he or she is going to be born into a world known to be dangerous. At the same time, the effects of trauma are enormous and long lasting: 'shattering, devastating, causing internal disruption by putting ego function mediation out of action' (Freud, 1967), impacting on the next generation in the family as well as those more immediately affected.

Clearly, survivors enter parenthood at different points in the resolution of their own abuse and, depending on this and the degree of the effects of the abuse, they will experience parenting differently. Pregnancy, birth and motherhood, particularly in the early years of childhood, inevitably make women vulnerable physically and emotionally. Mothers need to trust that medical interventions in pregnancy and beyond are necessary and will be carried out professionally and sensitively rather than invasively and inappropriately; and that partners and other central figures will be supportive and caring. Even for the most independent of women, pregnancy and motherhood at least temporarily entrusts them to a state of increased dependence on others and brings into being a small person who is intrinsically dependent. For the survivor mother, both the state of becoming a parent and the existence of a child can thrust her back into earlier anxieties about trust and dependency. Given these can be experienced by many mothers as they make the enormous shift from selfhood to motherhood, it is hardly surprising that they are highlighted for women who have had their trust shattered and for whom dependency led to danger, damage and pain.

Many women who suffered abuse experienced highly ambivalent relationships with their abuser: perpetrators are skilled at declaring love and interpreting abusive acts as both desired by the victim and as being a legitimate expression of love. Survivors can grow up believing there is a cost to being 'loved' as a child, confused as to the meaning of love, and knowing that those whom society believes to be trustworthy are often not so. Survivors often also grow up having considerable difficulty in recognizing or trusting their own judgement. So often this has been denied or distorted in childhood as perpetrators re-frame abuse into acts that are described as 'loving' or as 'deserved', and the wider world can reinforce this denial by neither seeing nor hearing. Abuse destroys the central core of the person – the ability to trust oneself and others. With this as the backdrop to motherhood and partnership it is small wonder that it can be hard for a survivor to trust her partner. In the question, we do not know the history of this woman's adult relationships. For some survivors the shadow of childhood abuse hangs over them into adulthood and other abusive relationships follow, whilst others manage to shift this pattern. For the former group, anxieties are likely to be especially high, particularly if initially these relationships began non-abusively and hopefully.

It is important to note that we are told here that this woman's anxieties are 'irrational'; but they may not be, and the counsellor has to achieve a balance between exploring these anxieties as a consequence of abuse, and checking out if there is a real basis for such worries. Some women cannot bear to acknowledge that their partner may be an abuser, since the guilt and shame feel intolerable, but for some this is the reality. A further complexity might be that the client herself has concerns that she could abuse her child, and is unconsciously projecting these anxieties on to her partner. Many parents who have been abused are very aware of the 'cycle of abuse', which adds to the losses of abuse by instilling the fear that they too in their turn will abuse their children. So for any counsellor faced with this scenario it is important to unravel the source of the anxiety. It is too simplistic to fall into a reassuring mode.

However, if the counsellor is as sure as she can be that these fears are unfounded in reality there are several avenues that can be helpful to explore. Helping the client to understand the source of these worries can begin to give her back her own power. To be able to understand, challenge and change one's own response can be empowering and reinforce the adult abilities and judgement in the client. Some survivors have not recognized how their own boundaries were decimated in childhood, and the ongoing impact of this in terms of not trusting others. Similarly, there is little experience of difficult feelings – so often present when caring for children – as capable of being safely contained. Knowing that feelings and actions are not necessarily the same thing is often illuminating. These crucial distinctions are blurred by abuse: the nature of abusive experiences is that the perpetrator acts on desires and feelings rather than appropriately containing and dealing with them. Everything is spilled on to the child. Recognizing that feelings can be felt, owned and acknowledged, dealt with and safely contained, and need not be emptied on to others, can be crucial.

Trusting a partner with a child is particularly problematic if the partner does not know about the abuse, or if a previous partner actually has abused the child. Exploring that relationship with the client is particularly important. Some have told their partners about the abuse, and the partner may be supportive, but not necessarily aware of these types of anxieties – indeed they are difficult concerns to share. Sometimes it is appropriate and helpful to work with the couple, so that anxieties and fears can be explored and contained in the therapeutic setting. It can be helpful for the non-abused partner to be given information and explanations in terms of the impact of abuse. Many have no idea of the extent of it, and that their partner's fears are quite normal responses to having experienced the abnormal. However, if they know, they can play a key role in helping to work through anxieties and difficulties, although some may need help themselves to do so. It is surprising how many partners of survivors do not know about the abuse, or have only a sketchy version of it and its effects. Sometimes they may know something is wrong but have little idea of its precise nature. Abuse survivors are very used to having to keep secrets, and have been brought up in an environment that is not conducive to clear and straightforward communication. They may think they have been communicative to their partner, but when this is explored with both this is genuinely not the case. Partners can feel quite overwhelmed when they see the fuller picture, and experience their own feelings of loss, inadequacy, guilt and shame, which in turn need to be addressed.

The anxiety in the client in this question is not unusual and can result in complex manoeuvring in which the parent has to find ways and means to avoid leaving the child alone with the partner. Bath times and bed times may seem especially dangerous. One mother described how when her husband was bathing their 3-year-old daughter she would creep quietly up the stairs and suddenly appear in the bathroom, just to check, but trying to pass it off as a game of peek-a-boo. This understandably irritated her husband and perplexed the little girl, who asked her daddy why mummy was jumping around the door like a jack-in-the-box, and why she looked so worried. Another parent described how if her husband got out of bed to go to the toilet at night she would always follow him to make sure he did not go into the child's bedroom; and how she would never let herself go to sleep until she was sure her husband was asleep.

There is an obvious effect on the partnerships in these examples, but the anxiety was also being communicated to the children. These mothers could rationally say that they knew their partners were trustworthy, and it seemed that this was accurate; but at another level deep anxieties existed. They could not trust their own judgement that these were non-abusive men. In their history, people who had been deemed to be trustworthy were not. The secrecy of abuse was being perpetuated, and the unspoken fear of these mothers that nowhere was safe produced anxiously attached children, who had difficulties in separating. In the first example, it was only possible for that mother to move forward by helping her place and understand the source of her anxieties, recognize the complexities of her relationship with her daughter that directly arose from the abuse (Walker, 1999), share much of this with her partner, and face the extreme damage the abuse had done to her ability to trust. A key aspect was helping her to recognize and hold to her own judgements of people and situations, which were frequently extremely accurate and perceptive. She also painfully recognized her own need to keep her daughter very close to her and her difficulty in allowing anyone else to be part of this relationship. In time this began to change, and the welcome birth of another child marked very real changes for her, her relationship with her partner and her children.

* * *

2.3 I have a male client who knows that he was abused regularly by an uncle, but every attempt he has made as an adult to tell his parents has met with disbelief. It seems to me very important to him that he is believed. Am I right? How can I help him understand his parents' reaction?

Survivors often express their need both to be believed by those who are close to them and to have the perpetrator acknowledge their actions and apologize. Sadly, many survivors have to come to terms with the reality that neither will happen. This does not mean that they cannot or will not be believed by others, nor that such belief is also deeply significant, although the experience of some is of disbelief piled upon disbelief, or of being blamed for the abuse: 'I had tried telling aunties, but they'd talk to my mother and it would cause more trouble. I was never believed and I'd end up being called a liar and all sorts' (Walker, 1992: 101). Many have written about the helpfulness of the client telling their story and being believed (Herman, 1992; Salter, 1995). Salter notes that the client 'cannot heal in the absence of emotional visibility. Reality is indeed a consensual experience, and the client's view of herself must be validated by another for it to take hold' (Salter, 1995: 262). So what also may be extremely important for this client is to know that the counsellor believes him, thus validating the client's belief in himself and his experiences. However, it should be remembered that being believed in itself triggers conflicting emotions. Hall and Lloyd (1989) quote a survivor who captures this vividly: 'I want you to believe because these terrible things really did happen to me, but if you believe, I will have to face up to them and that might be even worse for me' (1989: 107).

The counsellor's belief in this client may be the basis for their relationship and a crucial part of the recovery process, but nevertheless much work remains to be done. The key issue may not be helping the client to understand his parents' reaction, but rather understanding the significance for him of both telling his parents and wanting to be believed. Indeed, survivors often have their own clear and horribly accurate views on why their parents refused or still refuse to face the truth, and the counsellor should not assume that this client has not formulated his own opinions. Clients who are asked how they make sense of parental refusal to believe often offer the following: 'If they believed me they'd feel bad and they can't face that'; 'They think I lie and am bad and that he (the perpetrator) is good'; 'They'd have to take some action and they won't'; 'Other children in the family may be implicated and they don't want to know'; 'They'd feel guilty and ashamed – they'd rather blame me'; 'She (or he) was abused by him as well'; 'They're frightened, and they don't want to split the family up'.

However, others have not reached this point but tenaciously feel that if only they explain better or more clearly, or just keep on trying, they will get the acknowledgement that they need. And for some this is the case and indeed it brings the best results. When they communicate their experience clearly and honestly, the truth is acknowledged and support is forthcoming. But as therapists and counsellors, it is important to recognize that this is a relatively rare event and that clients are more likely to encounter just the opposite response.

In working with this client to make sense of his need for parental acknowledgement, it must be recognized that this scenario touches on extremely complex dynamics. Recognizing that a refusal to believe is not the fault of the victim but is the responsibility of these parents can be helpful and liberating to the client; but it can also be intensely problematic and painful: children need to see their parents as benign and caring and they engage in psychological manoeuvrings to maintain them in this role, which continue into adulthood. Therefore, redefining refusal to believe as the parents' problem, rather than indicating that they themselves are flawed or bad, is not straightforward. As an adult it can be intensely painful to give up on the belief of good parents who did not know but who would have acted if they did. Working with the client to grieve this loss is a painstaking process. To face the fact that parents have betrayed you through not believing, and that other considerations – like keeping the family together – are more important to them than the welfare of the survivor, is a deeply isolating and alienating experience. However, ultimately it is one that frees the survivor from clinging hopefully to relationships that will never provide what is wanted or needed. It can also provide the route to a realistic appraisal of what parents are able to give. Survivors then have a choice of deciding whether (or not) something is better than nothing. If at the same time letting go of the parents allows for the development of other relationships, real steps forward can be made. For some survivors, going through this process faces them with other stark truths, commonly that parents knew about the abuse, or suspected all along and did not intervene.

It is important to validate that this client has a right to expect his parents to believe him, but also to consider how he can begin to move on if this is not forthcoming. Exploring his perceptions of what would change if he is believed can be useful: expectations can be unrealistic, and it is helpful to name and to know these. This can be potentially empowering for the client as he recognizes his hopes and needs and begins to assess these against the reality of his situation. Survivors frequently want resolution and hope for apology, confirmation, acknowledgement and healing. They may see acknowledgement of the truth as an essential and extremely significant event and step, and expect their parents to rally around and support the survivor.

As noted earlier, belief and validation is crucial to the survivor, but even if the parents in this example do 'believe' it may come as a disappointment to the client if either he has attached too much significance to this, or if the parents somehow fail to react sufficiently. The parents may acknowledge the truth, but this in itself may not make it all better. Sometimes apparent belief is mitigated by rationalization: 'Surely it wasn't that bad'; 'It's a long time ago now – it shouldn't have happened but let's put it behind us'; 'You were so young, it wouldn't have done much harm'; 'You just have to forget it and get on with your life': these are all responses I have heard. If too many hopes have been attached to being believed, there may be a real sense of anti-climax and the thought 'I've done that, now what?'.

When adult survivors confront parents with the truth of their abuse it is a situation that is potentially multi-faceted. There is the obvious hope for belief, validation and support. Abused children who cannot tell their parents frequently feel they have lost them; they have become psychological orphans, estranged and lost. They lose the belief that parents will keep them safe, and will know what is important, what is happening and when things are wrong; that they will be able to intervene and will essentially keep the world at bay until the child is ready to be exposed to it, and able to cope with it in increasingly bigger doses as they grow older. Abuse is totally disillusioning. The world as a safe enough place and parents as good enough disappears. Children's growing disillusion with parents as all knowing, all powerful and all loving is a normal developmental theme, particularly evident in adolescence when the loving and loved parent is often turned into the equivalent of the parent from hell. This is age-appropriate (albeit perplexing for the parent), but quite different from having illusion snatched away brutally at too early an age. So it is not surprising that the abused child as he or she grows up may want to reclaim some of the territory that has been stolen in childhood, and find parental closeness and attachment.

However, other aspects exist too. One is the rage that the child, and subsequently the adult can feel towards the non-seeing, non-knowing parents. Davies and Frawley note that 'one can speculate, in fact, whether child sexual abuse could extend over time if parents were awake, attached, and attuned to their children's behaviors and emotional life' (1994: 168). Adult survivors can wonder the same, and their attempts to make their parents believe can arise from a desire to punish them, to make them suffer as they have suffered, to experience guilt, shame and despair as the child victim has done and the adult survivor may still experience. It is perhaps not surprising that parents who did not recognize that their child was being abused may also in later life not recognize the extent of the damage, or be fully emotionally available to their adult offspring. For the survivor losses can be further exacerbated if an attempt to seek revenge by demanding and expecting belief also fails. For other survivors, telling parents can represent the desire for reparation rather than revenge. This is most likely to be the case when the survivor has worked through the impact of the abuse and has reached a psychological plateau where some considerable degree of ease with the abuse and with the self has occurred. In this instance wanting to tell parents can represent a desire to rebuild some contact and regain some lost connections. The truth can be told with the assurance that the survivor has moved on and is therefore not looking to the parents to make it all better. In this scenario there can be a desire that there should be no more secrets, combined with a much greater realism regarding possible outcomes.

In working with a client to deal with the situation in this question it is essential to explore the variety of unconscious and conscious motivations that may be at play. This is in the context of understanding the plethora of losses that arise not only from the abuse but also from having parents who, for whatever reasons, did not 'know'.

* * *

2.4 My client says that she thinks she was abused as a very young child, but as far as I can see there is no actual evidence for this – no memory, no one has told her this, etc. What can I make of this suggestion? And how should I respond to it?

Enormous care has to be taken in responding to such a presentation. In this situation, where the client may be searching for a cause for her current distress, it is unhelpful to her to collude in what could be a false assumption on her part. This will not only prevent the exploration of other meanings for her unhappiness, it could also be deeply misleading for the client and for her family. However, this does not mean she was not abused, or that the counsellor is not be open to this possibility; but if this was at a very young age, actual memories are unlikely to be present.

In this instance it can help the client to explore why she thinks this is so: if there are no memories and no one has told her this, where are these thoughts and feelings coming from? Is she experiencing sensations in her body, or feelings or thoughts that are confusing? When she did start thinking this? Was there a trigger, either external or internal? Was it at a time of crisis or transition in her life? It can be helpful to build up a picture of the client's life and relationships to see if any clues lie in the patterns thus revealed. It is crucial to be open to all possibilities, but to be suggestive of none. A central aspect of a counsellor's or therapist's practice is to be able to tolerate uncertainty, to cope with not knowing, and to begin to help the client also to manage not knowing. In the situation described here, the client may never know in a definitive sense the truth of her early experiences, but she can be helped to live with this uncertainty and the realities of her present life.

Two examples spring to mind. One was of a deeply unhappy young woman. She struggled to unravel the causes of this and commented that she sometimes thought she must have been abused, and indeed wished she had been, as this would give her something tangible to which to attach her distress. Her mother had died at an early age, and her life thereafter had been complex, unpredictable and unsettled. Boundaries and relationships had been unclear and her world was marked by a lack of reliable care. There was no evidence of abuse, but plenty of a lifestyle that was not geared to the needs of a child, in which she experienced conflicting demands upon her, and often felt a burden and a nuisance. There could never be any certainty that in this world of ever-changing people she had not been abused. But what was clear was that the experiences she did recall and were verifiable had been disturbing, disruptive and not conducive to facilitating her growth as a person. Unravelling these experiences was profoundly upsetting for her, but also ultimately gave her relief and the ability to move on in her life, recognizing that some aspects of her childhood were going to remain hazy.

The other example relates to a 19-year-old man who was self-harming and very depressed. His self-harming intensified in any situation in which he became close to anyone, so counselling was intrinsically experienced by him as dangerous. He recalled quite clearly physical abuse from his stepfather in his early school years, and this was reluctantly acknowledged by his mother. It was only much later in the work that he discovered from seeing his medical notes that his father had abused him as a baby, and that the evidence of this had been used in divorce proceedings. This was both an extreme shock but also gave him a sense of something fitting, of a missing piece being supplied. It is unusual that evidence of very early abuse is revealed and confirmed in so clear a way, and it is important to note that although it did help make sense of his presentation, therapeutic work would and could have continued without this knowledge. It would, of course, not have been the same; but it is impossible to say if it would have been more or less successful. Even without this information his counsellor already felt that he was very likely to have been damaged in some way at a very young age, because of the way he presented. It is possible to work therapeutically in a way that is appropriate to early damage, without having precise knowledge as to the events of that time.

In work with any client it is important to listen to, and validate their experience as being real to them. However, it is not always the case that feelings, however real, are necessarily linked to events as perceived by the client. It is this process of carefully exploring without assumption or prejudice that is core to the therapeutic process, as is the ability to stay with uncertainty, and to help the client to do so. This can be done whilst acknowledging that not remembering, or not having evidence, does not mean either that abuse did take place, or that it did not.

* * *

2.5 I have a client I have worked with for some months who is suddenly determined to confront her abuser. I want to respect her wishes but feel she is bound to be further hurt. Can confronting abusers help survivors?

Clients who express a strong desire to confront their abuser may have many different reasons for doing so. Some want a definite resolution, others an apology, others a confirmation and acknowledgement from the abuser that the abuse did take place, and others see confrontation as a step in the healing process. Survivors may see this as an essential and extremely significant step, and some will describe how they have always dreamed of doing this, sometimes accompanied by a sense of being unable to rest until the confrontation has taken place. They hope this will give them back the sense of control over their self that was so decimated by the abuse. Others clearly want revenge: they want to shock the perpetrator; they long to see horror and fear on their face, and want the abuser to suffer. In addition, the survivor may feel that confrontation, if the abuser was a family member, will somehow cause their wider family to rally round and support the survivor, and that they will finally understand.

The consequences of confrontation can be very different from what is longed for. Even if the abuser does acknowledge, apologize, or confirm the abuse, it can still be a disappointment to the survivor. It does not simply make it all better, and the survivor may anyway suspect, often correctly, the genuineness of the abuser. Abusers do not easily acknowledge abuse or feel real sorrow: denial and refusal to take responsibility is the more likely response. There is a strong likelihood that confronting abusers makes clients feel worse rather than better: old fears and memories can be reawakened, and unhelpful and old patterns of behaving can re-emerge, especially if the survivor is not able to contain their own feelings. The survivor can feel that yet again everything is out of their control, and that whatever they do does not work. They may get angry and distressed when they had wanted to be cool and calm and in control.

Similarly, the wider family may not suddenly become supportive, but instead close ranks and not believe; or they may believe but not actually give any support. Statements such as 'It's no good digging up the past', 'He's an old man now why upset him', or 'You must learn to move on and put these things behind you' are frequently reported by survivors as responses they have received.

Another consequence is that family members can be genuinely deeply distressed, and for some survivors this creates feelings of guilt, particularly if those persons are themselves elderly and vulnerable. This was the experience of a survivor abused by her grandfather. She confronted him when he and her grandmother were in their late seventies. Although grandfather did acknowledge some of the abuse, he also minimized it and accused his granddaughter of inviting and enjoying his attentions. This in itself distressed her, but the pain of her grandmother who witnessed this encounter was such that she wished she had remained quiet. This reflected her childhood experience when she was told not to tell – and that if she did she would destroy the family.

There are many issues when clients are considering confronting abusers. Whilst it is important not to collude with plans that appear ill considered, it is also crucial to respect the client and not become destructive or controlling. What is needed is to help the client to consider all the options and their possible consequences, whilst at the same time validating their right to take their own decisions. It can be hard for counsellors to contain and deal with their own anxieties and difficult feelings in this situation: it can feel to counsellors as if they are wishing to restrict a client's newly found autonomy. It does help the client to work on preparing for 'worst scenarios', although it is important that this is done without the client feeling that the therapist is simply being negative, or is somehow not on their side. It is a necessary skill to gently but firmly challenge the client who feels that confronting will make it all better, whilst also exploring and acknowledging any negative feelings this might produce towards the counsellor.

If the client experiences the counsellor as essentially being on their side in making this decision, rather than feeling in opposition, this opens up the possibility of real exploration and discussion. Acknowledging what a major decision it is, and checking out with the client if he or she is able to make a space to think, is important. It can help to remind the client that the abusive experience was always out of her or his control, and that taking sufficient time now is a way of reclaiming this. Working with the client on such an issue includes exploring a range of possible consequences, including the worst, and thinking how to prepare for these; helping look at what he or she really hopes to get from confrontation, looking at what may be realistic and what is more likely fantasy, and considering if there are other routes to achieve what he or she wants. All this helps to ground this problematic area.

It is, however, important to recognize, even if it seems ill-considered and likely to end in tears, that the survivor may still need to go ahead. Ultimately, this must be her or his decision; and even if the consequences are deeply problematic and distressing it may be something the survivor needs to do. And for some people confronting their abuser does have positive consequences in the longer term, even if it is very upsetting in the short term. Whatever the consequences, if the client chooses to go ahead, he or she must know that the counsellor is there to help deal with it and that there is respect for such a decision.

For some, the consequences of confronting are more positive. In my experience the latter is most likely to result when, paradoxically, least is expected. A survivor who confronted her abusive father was left feeling genuinely triumphant and released from a great burden. She chose to telephone him, recognizing that facing him would make her vulnerable again. She had carefully planned what to say and how to say it. She began by clearly stating that she knew he would always deny what he had done, and that she had no need for him to say otherwise, and no belief that he was capable of owning to it. She continued by listing what he had done to her, and made it clear that she wanted no response from him. What she had needed was to hear herself say the words. In exploring this beforehand she felt the worst scenario would be that he would put the phone down, in which case she intended to keep trying; and if he persisted she would write to him in his workplace, sending it by recorded delivery. It is important to note that this was something she had thought about, and discussed at length with her therapist. Other survivors would handle the same situation differently. The main objective is to help each individual to find their own way through this situation, so that it is ultimately helpful rather than destructive, and changes rather than repeats old patterns with abusers.

When a client who has been in therapy for some time presents unexpectedly with a strong desire to confront their abuser it is also worth considering if this relates to the therapeutic relationship. Might the client

want to confront the therapist with something? Could it be that the counsellor has not heard them sufficiently well? It is important not to assume
that such a wish must be related to the work, whilst bearing in mind it is a
possibility, and so to carefully monitor and reflect on the process.
Another aspect to consider is that, for many survivors, however much they
may dream of confronting their abuser, and somehow thereby both con-
quer and control them, they have to find another route. One such way is
to confront the abuser within them, and to so work on what they feel
about and need to say to an inner persecuting and abusive voice. In this
way it is important to recognize that confronting abusers is not always a
process of dealing with them face to face in a literal sense, but can be a
process that takes place within the survivor and between them and their
counsellor.

* * *

2.6 Sometimes clients refer to sex games in which they were 'abused' by older children, sometimes siblings. Clients are unsure, and so am I, when sexual play between children becomes abuse.

Interest in their own bodies, and the bodies of others, is a normal part of
the developing child's world. Similarly, sexual experimentation, manifest-
ing itself in different forms at different times of development, is also part
of the growing child and young person's quest for identity. Yates (1991)
describes how during the pre-school years peer sex play and exhibitionism
are common, whilst during early school years children share sexual jokes
and often engage in sex play amongst their own gender. Such experimentation carried out within a peer group, or same age pairing, carries with it
a mutuality of curiosity and discovery, and often of playfulness. It is this
mutuality, based on an equality of developmental level, of power and of
choice, combined with an unspoken knowledge and awareness of how far
the game or experimentation will go, that renders such activity generally
harmless rather than harmful. In this context a child can be playing but can
also stop when he or she wishes to. In other words, the play, to use the questioner's words, is 'between' them; it is not imposed upon them.
    There is a world of difference between small children happily playing
'doctors and nurses', or 'mummies and daddies', and a situation where an
older child, or children, forces, coerces or persuades a younger child, for
example, 'to find out what daddies do'. These scenarios can be accompanied by actual force, or threats of force, or threats that harm will come

to the smaller child or those they love (including their pets) if the child either tells, makes a noise, or fights back. The child attackers are therefore behaving like adult perpetrators. Older children can and do abuse younger children, and the effects on the child can be as damaging as abuse by an adult. Indeed, to a small child the difference is possibly academic: bigger people have power physically and psychologically whether the age difference is five or twenty-five years. We need to remember that, to a child, another child who is only a year or two older can be a very awesome figure.

The reality that child abuse is carried out by older children is reflected in clinical practice in working with survivors, where this is a frequently presented issue, and in research findings on sex offenders. Abel and Rouleau (1990) found that a significant number of paedophiles in their study had demonstrated deviant behaviour prior to the age of 18, and that for many this was at an even younger age. Freund and Kuban (1993) found that many sex offenders start offending in their teens. Many of these young abusers (Johnson, 1993) will have been abused themselves: one effect of child sexual abuse is to increase sexualized behaviour, which in turn can become acted out against smaller and vulnerable children.

Reports of sibling abuse are common clinically, and Jacobs notes that 'among the most pervasive forms of re-victimisation reported by the respondents in childhood and adolescence are incestuous assaults from male siblings and/or other male relatives' (1994: 105). Sibling abuse seems to be particularly confusing for their victims, as many recognized in the research, because the abusing sibling was also being abused himself or herself. A young woman recalling the physical and emotional abuse perpetrated by her older sister commented that she saw her sister being very violently treated by her stepfather and she witnessed her pain and distress. Even at a young age she had some insight into why her sister treated her so badly, and she had some sympathy with her, whilst simultaneously being terrified of her and of what she could and did do to her. However, what caused her the greatest distress was watching her sister abuse an even younger sibling. Whilst she could apparently cope with knowing that she could not stop her sister abusing her, she could not live easily with the knowledge that she had not protected her younger sister.

Children in this situation are triple losers: they are attacked by their sibling whilst often witnessing abuse being perpetrated against that sibling by one parent, at the same time living with the reality that the non-abusing parent is not going to intervene to help anyone. In the example above, the mother was physically present but psychologically absent. She often literally witnessed what was occurring but failed to actually be present in any real sense. This young woman described her mother as 'there but not there; real but ghostlike; alive but frozen', thus adding further to her confusion and isolation.

In my work with survivors it does appear that there is very real likelihood of sibling abuse not being taken seriously either at the time, or when help is sought later. It needs to be recognized that older siblings can be as devious as adult perpetrators when it comes to hiding or denying the truth, and that apparently responsible adults in the family may be quite unable to intervene. It is also likely to be the case that sibling abuse is most likely to occur in families where adults either have little real presence or power, or where abuse is being perpetrated on the children by those adults.

It is also important to remember that both brothers and sisters can be abusive. Older sisters who are given inappropriate responsibility for the care of younger children may be particularly likely to abuse, especially in a context where they themselves do not have sufficient boundaries placed on their behaviour, or where they too are being abused. A young woman described how, with a mother with serious mental health problems and a father who was an alcoholic, her older sister became almost entirely responsible for her. This older sister would vacillate between attempts to be caring, and outbreaks of extreme rage during which she would physically assault her little sister and threaten her if she told; in actual fact there was noone left to tell. This young woman had recently found out that her sister herself been sexually abused by a neighbour's son who was left in charge of her when she was 10 and he was 14. In this family no adult care was available: boundaries were broken, children were expected to take on adult responsibilities and a deeply abusive situation resulted.

Finally, it is worth pointing out that when people recall memories and events relating to the type of incidents alluded to here, they are often very able themselves to distinguish between abusive acts and playful, mutual experimentation. However, what can confuse the picture for them is the message the older child abuser might have given them. As with older perpetrators, the abuse is denied by describing it as a game that is to be enjoyed, or as something the child has invited, or that is the fault of the victim. We know from research (Becker et al., 1986) that adolescent abusers are unlikely to admit to what they have done. As Salter comments: 'The denial of a sex offender sometimes strains the credulity of the most gullible' (Salter, 1995: 6). This is as true of young offenders as it is of those who are older. It may also be the case that we find it difficult to believe that children are capable of horrific acts of violence and perversion, and prefer to frame such behaviour as harmless play and experimentation. However, once again that view can lead to survivors not being heard.

CHAPTER 3

Effects of abuse on the adult survivor

3.1 I have heard it said that clients with eating problems, or with alcohol and drug problems, have probably been abused. Is that right?

Whilst it should never be assumed that a client presenting with eating, alcohol or drug problems has been abused, both research and the experience of those working with clients with these difficulties suggest that there is a strong relationship. All of these could be regarded as self-harming behaviours. Both Oppenheimer et al. (1985) and Palmer et al. (1990) note the connection between childhood abuse and eating disorders, and certainly the language used by clients when they describe their eating behaviour is often reminiscent of the abusive experiences. For example, a young bulimic woman abused by her father described how she forced the food into herself without any feeling that she could control what was being forced into her. She went on to explain the relief and feeling of power when she was able to vomit the food out. Another young woman who was anorexic, who had been abused by several men in her family, described how triumphant she felt over saying no to food: this was something that at last she had absolute control over.

Difficulties with food have many meanings for abuse survivors: they may reflect a disgust with femininity and sexuality; both lack of eating and severe over-eating disguise these aspects of self. Abuse survivors can also feel much safer with a body that is not obviously and attractively sexual. In addition, shame and guilt are often created by abuse, and not eating or over-eating are both self-punitive. For those who have been the subject of such cruel control in their childhood, controlling food both as adolescents and as adults may be their only experience of controlling their lives and their bodies. For others, particularly anorexics, not eating can be less related to self-punishment but more to punishing the abuser: an indirect and passively angry statement of the damage that has been done to them. It

41

also needs to be remembered that abused children often experience great difficulty in eating: they are too tense, unhappy and anxious, and this can be reflected in the adult experience. Food cannot simply be a pleasure – it is associated with anxiety and unhappiness.

There is also a close link between substance abuse and childhood abuse. Herman (1981) found that 35 per cent of her sample of incest survivors abused both drugs and alcohol; and Jehu et al. (1984) estimate that 41 per cent of survivors abused alcohol. Hall and Lloyd discuss the connection between substance use and childhood abuse: 'Many incest survivors have never learned appropriate ways of dealing with their anger and frequently turn it on themselves. This leads to self mutilation, alcohol and drug abuse' (1989: 50). Workers in agencies dealing with drug and alcohol abusers report more and more frequently a connection between childhood abuse and later drug and alcohol abuse: one suggested to me that at least 90 per cent of users of a drugs counselling service are survivors of childhood abuse.

Not only do drugs and alcohol serve to numb and block the pain temporarily and induce a feeling of goodwill or oblivion; they can effectively also block out the attempts of others to help. They are an effective barrier to relationships and as such serve many purposes. They prevent the survivor being in touch with his or her pain; they prevent anyone else getting too close; they express both a rage towards the perpetrator and the hopelessness and helplessness of the abused child, and also reflect and express the lack of containment and boundaries so inherent in abuse. Additionally, abuse survivors often feel different, alienated and marginalized; they feel as if they have lived and suffered in another world where different rules have been operating. As a result there can be a powerful attraction to groups and activities that are similarly marginalized, carry a stigma and are seen as anti-social. They feel they do not fit the mainstream world, but others who run risks and skirmish with danger can be deeply attractive and appealing. Not only do they match the survivor's sense of difference, inadequacy, shame and non-belonging, but being allied with them can also be a way of expressing rage towards and disappointment in mainstream society, which was meant to protect them but singularly failed to do so. There is a further aspect to this that is anxiety provoking for those who work with survivors who are also substance abusing: such a lifestyle in itself puts survivors at greater risk of further abuse.

* * *

3.2 What impact does abuse have on the survivor as a parent, and on the next generation of children? And how can counselling help?

Clearly, survivors enter parenthood at different points in the resolution of their own abuse, and depending on this and the degree of the effects of the abuse, they will experience parenting differently. However, some patterns of difficulties for them and their children are identifiable. The cycle of abuse (see Question 2.1) is perhaps the best known, but there are other subtler patterns that are more difficult to define, recognise and identify. However, these are also crucial to survivors and their children, creating complexities and anxieties in their relationships. This cycle of abuse, whilst significant, is in danger of being overstated. The mythology that abuse breeds abuse in itself causes survivors considerable anxiety, and it is crucial to recognize that large numbers of survivors do not abuse their children either actively or passively. For the many abuse survivors who have children and do not abuse them, this in itself can be their pride and joy, a measure of their ability to do things differently, and to make things change. But relationships in respect of their children can still be complex, and sometimes problematic. Being a parent is not easy in the best of circumstances and a history of abuse is clearly not the ideal preparation for parenthood.

For some abuse survivors difficulties in regard to children start before they are even conceived and continue thereafter. Survivors may experience powerful ambivalence during pregnancy and beyond – they long for the child, but he or she is being born into a world known to be dangerous. Some say they will not have children. This decision can result from extreme and as yet unresolved difficulties around intimacy and sexuality; gynaecological damage caused by the abuse may literally mean they cannot bear children; others are terrified that they too will abuse. And so the losses from abuse are piled one upon the other. Conversely, there can be an overwhelming desire for a child. A baby provides hope and the potential for restoring normal family life that many fear their abuse has destroyed. The parent may have high hopes and expectations in respect of the child, but also many fears and anxieties.

During pregnancy a woman who has been penetratively sexually abused can experience the growing baby as an invasion of her body and the re-creation of the abusive experience. Abuse frequently deprives a woman of her own mother, whom she may long for at such a time. The scans and intimate examinations that accompany pregnancy, as well as the birth itself, may be profoundly disturbing. For some the actual birth of a child precipitates the return of memories, or the painful highlighting of those hazily held but never faced. There may be particular difficulties if a child is wanted but post-natal depression results. There may be a sense of the inevitability of things going wrong. The anxieties of survivors at this crucial time has important implications for intervening therapeutically, and counsellors, therapists and others involved in the care of parents and young children need to be aware of how crucial therapeutic input can be to ensure the emotional health of all those concerned.

Wanting and having a baby is of course only the beginning. A woman in her twenties had difficulty accepting any negative feelings towards her very much wanted 18-month-old baby. For this young mother a crucial step forward was in recognizing the difference between feelings and acting them out, and between fantasy and reality. These distinctions had been blurred and eroded by her own abuse. The nature of her abusive experiences had been that the perpetrator had acted on, and acted out, desires, difficult feelings and experiences rather than appropriately containing them and dealing with them. Everything was spilt on to her as a child. Recognizing that it was both acceptable and understandable not being able to stand her screaming baby, and becoming confident that such feelings did not have to be acted out, was deeply illuminating for her. As with other abuse survivors she had little experience of ambivalent feelings being safely and responsibly contained.

A child reaching an age or stage that is significant for the parent – for instance, when they themselves were abused – can trigger powerful feelings and difficulties. A woman who had found mothering a pleasurable and fulfilling experience found that this changed apparently dramatically when her daughter became 13. She became anxious and found it very difficult to allow her daughter any freedom: she could not trust that her daughter could be safe in the wider world. Her daughter resented this and their relationship deteriorated. The mother was re-experiencing her own experiences as a 13-year-old of sexual abuse by a neighbour. Although this was always in her conscious memory, at another level it had not been dealt with; factual memories had become dissociated from deeply painful feelings, which were re-awakened by her daughter reaching the same age. Two aspects in counselling had particular significance: the first was the mother reconnecting the memories with the feelings and working these through; and the second was recognizing and exploring how at 13 the abuse led to the emotional loss of her own mother. She now feared experiencing a repeat of the devastation of losing her daughter through her need for autonomy and separateness. Only when she had dealt with these aspects was she able to begin to separate her own experiences from her daughter's and respond to her rather more effectively. At that stage she was also able to allow her husband a more active involvement. She was able to recognize how previously she had excluded him from parenting.

During adolescence the combination of challenging boundaries, the need for autonomy and the experience of powerful feelings, including anger, can make this a highly charged time both for the children of survivors of abuse and for their parents. The dilemma of placing appropriate boundaries without being overly restrictive, and being sufficiently relaxed and allowing space without giving so much that the child drowns in it or is poorly cared for, is a difficult balance to achieve in the best of circumstances. A history of trauma in the parent can make this a deeply anxious time. It is very easy to be either over-protective and over-anxious, warning too strongly of the dangers of the world and so becoming too restrictive; or to be so scared of being invasive, controlling and misusing parental power that the child is not held safely enough, expects instant gratification and never learns to handle frustration.

One survivor described how in her anxiety not to repeat the physical abuse of her father, she allowed her daughter and her son virtually total freedom: she could not say no to them for fear of becoming abusive and repressive. She felt that in their teens they were becoming like the abusive grandfather, and that her anxiety not to be abusive had recreated a cycle via another route. Her daughter in particular was becoming violent, abusive and uncontrollable. This mother's distress was enormous; her ability to say no appropriately was non-existent, so that helping her to re-establish sensible boundaries was vital.

Teenage years are notoriously difficult. Another mother, who had been severely physically and emotionally abused and had learnt from an early age that complete compliance was the way to avoid worse abuse, became very distressed when her 13-year-old daughter changed from a lovable little girl to an assertive young woman who could be argumentative, secretive and difficult. Helping her to understand the normality of this adolescent presentation was like turning a light on for her. She had no idea that adolescence is often like that.

It can also be difficult for a parent who has been abused to trust a partner with a child. This is a particular problem if the partner does not know about the abuse, or if a previous partner actually has abused the child. Examples of such difficulties are given in the answer to Question 2.2. Other variations of this pattern are parents, particularly fathers but also mothers, who are scared to cuddle or touch their children, or allow them even as very small children to get into the parental bed in case this action is misconstrued as abusive. The losses of abuse can once again be seen to pile up for both the parent and the child.

A further parental dilemma for abuse survivors who are parents is whether or not to tell their child of their own abuse. This is particularly significant when the abuser has been a close family member and when they are still involved in the family. Parents worry that telling invades the child's innocence as theirs was invaded by the abuse; but conversely, many worry that if they keep silent they perpetuate the secrecy of the abuse and may not enable the child to protect himself or herself. It is apparent from parents that this is a minefield to steer through, since in terms of the impact on the child any information given has to be both manageable and age appropriate; and equally crucially it can be given only when parents have resolved their own issues sufficiently to enable them to contain the child so he or she will feel safely held.

The children of survivors are caught up in these dynamics: children expect to see other close family members, but when parents have been abused by them and the child has to be protected, then one resolution is for the child either to have no contact or only closely supervised contact. However, children ask questions, and sense the tension and anxieties, so that unspoken fantasies and ambivalent feelings arise. Breaking contact with abusive relatives does not totally solve the dilemma although it does protect the child. The child loses family members because cutting off the abuser often cuts off others in the family as well; children wonder why they are not allowed to visit by themselves, cannot have these family members to baby-sit, or go for holidays with them as other children do. If some contact is retained, yet parents are aware of the need to protect and supervise the child, this can be puzzling.

Others stay in contact because as yet they are unable to acknowledge what has happened – at some level they are in denial. They may fail to recognize the danger of leaving children with abusing relatives. A survivor described her disbelief that she had allowed her now grown-up children to stay unsupervised when young with their grandmother, who had brutally physically abused the mother as a child and remained explosive and unpredictable. Later in her life, having moved on through her counselling, she recognized that by providing the grandchildren in this way she had still been trying to please the mother in order to gain the maternal approval she still so desperately needed. She still did not get the approval – she had in her mother's eyes been a bad daughter and now she was also a bad mother.

Other children of abused parents end up just as isolated and alienated by their life situation as their parents did through the abuse. Parents who have been abused may have difficulty knowing what a child needs, having had no good model themselves. The child may have few friends, act or be treated age inappropriately, and be both over-protected and under-socialized. A young man in therapy was the only child of wealthy elderly parents who doted on him – he was their pride and joy and their only love and hope. Father had been emotionally abused and mother had been severely neglected as a child: they viewed the world as dangerous and smothered their son with care and money. Any distress or difficulty on his part had to be immediately removed. As a 21-year-old he was totally alienated from his own age group, having no idea how to relate or deal with anything even mildly uncomfortable. It is clear that children of survivors of childhood abuse can have a very particular preciousness ascribed to them: their very existence is proof of the triumph of survival. For some children such preciousness feels overwhelming even when more subtly expressed. It is particularly noticeable in single children where there are no siblings to share the emotional load. Such children may feel that to be truly separate they have to cut and run. The transitional period of adolescent comings and goings, until finally entering a more autonomous adult state, can be disrupted. However, this specialness can be marked by anxiety about a world that is felt to be dangerous to all their hopes and aspirations.

The struggle to place appropriate boundaries is evident throughout childhood, but is particularly highlighted both with toddlers and with adolescents – at both ages children are struggling in different developmental ways towards autonomy and separateness. The parent who has survived abuse may experience a powerful need to maintain the symbiotic bond of the mother–baby dyad and may unconsciously discourage individuation. The development of a separate sense of self can be experienced as a narcissistic injury to the survivor parent. Children's attempts to take charge of themselves or their environment can create feelings of anxiety and helplessness in the parents. One task of parenting is to help a child towards healthy separation. At adolescence and other transitional times parents who have closely invested in their children's lives can experience pain and mourning, and for an abuse survivor this may be intensified. The temporary loss of loving closeness, the passing of the secure parent–child world and the transitional crisis can bring survivors face to face with what had been lost and destroyed for them.

It is the pride and joy of many a survivor that they have had children and have not been abusive to them. The pleasure in being 'good enough' parents can be immense. However, there can be a desire to over-compensate, to be the best of parents, and to show how well they can fulfil that role. This can give a message to the child that everything must always be all right, something that is clearly not possible. Children need to know that difficulties arise but need not be disasters, that they can be overcome and everyone survives. The hopes and expectations for the children of survivors of childhood abuse often exist in a vacuum: there is no childhood experience to refer back to, and no parents to consult. It can be lonely. For survivors of abuse who have lived with their personal boundaries invaded, with repression and fear, and who know from bitter personal experience how awful human behaviour can be, parenthood can be both particularly hard to manage, whilst also immensely fulfilling. Counselling in the context of these inter-generational issues that extend beyond the 'cycle of abuse' can therefore provide a valuable opportunity to prevent anxieties and difficulties from spilling disastrously into yet another generation.

* * *

3.3 Does abuse create repression and dissociation? Is there a difference between them and would I be able to recognize them in any of my clients?

There is a complex theoretical debate around the difference between repression and dissociation that dates back to the nineteenth century and the work of Freud and Janet. Pierre Janet was the first to formulate a theory of dissociation and multiple personality in his discussion (1889) of 'successive existences'. Freud was familiar with the work of Janet, and some of Breuer and Freud's formulations in *Studies on Hysteria* (1895) were at that stage quite close to those of Janet. However, Freud went on to develop a different model of the mind, in which the concept of repression took a central place. Repression was described as a 'horizontal split' between conscious and unconscious, quite at odds with the 'vertical split' between separate aspects of consciousness discussed by Janet and also by Prince (1906/1957, 1914, 1919). Janet's concept of dissociation was overtaken by Freud's concept of repression – one of his four cornerstones of psychoanalysis.

Ferenczi expressed a different and challenging viewpoint to that of Freud, and in his famous and controversial paper written and presented in 1932 (although unpublished until 1955), he examined the effects of childhood sexual trauma on his patients. He argued that ongoing assault on the child creates fragmentation and splits within the child:

> If the shocks increase in number during the development of the child, the number and the various kinds of splits in the personality increase too, and soon it becomes extremely difficult to maintain contact without confusion with all the fragments each of which behaves as a separate personality yet does not know of even the existence of the others, fragmentation one would be justified in calling atomisation. (1955: 165)

Ferenczi's description is very similar to the extreme end of dissociation that is seen in multiple personality (see Question 3.4). Fairbairn (1952), who worked with children who had been victims of sexual assault in World War II, also developed a detailed psychoanalytic model of dissociation arguing that Freud's division into id, ego, and superego was only one possibility amongst others of a structure of the mind. More recently, Reviere notes that currently many acknowledge the existence of both repression and dissociation:

> While current thinking acknowledges both horizontal and vertical layers of consciousness, many explain their coexistence, and thus their distinctions, by concluding that the process of repression functions to manage both internally derived unacceptable material (e.g. impulses, wishes, aggressive

fantasies) and external stressors, while the process of dissociation serves primarily to manage external trauma. (Reviere, 1996: 25)

The theoretical debate continues, and notably becomes especially contentious when multiple personality is under discussion. It is part of an ongoing debate taking place in the context of other issues, for instance, relating to the effects of early trauma on memories.

Repression can be broadly defined as an unconscious process whereby frightening material is removed from awareness on a relatively permanent basis, although it can return, as in the instance of a survivor recovering memories of abuse. So, by the defence of repression, the ego is helped to gain control over painful or conflictual experiences and material, so that they are not allowed to enter conscious awareness. Dissociation can be seen as a continuum where it can be a pathological mechanism (at the extreme end of this is multiple personality) through to a healthily and normally adaptive defence. An object relations view of dissociation tends to think that it protects the person from overwhelming memories of traumatic events and preserves the internal object world of the abused child. Dissociation can also be understood as a state of auto-hypnosis whereby the pain and terror caused by the trauma is turned into relaxation, calmness, numbness and a feeling of disappearance. On one level, passivity and compliance occur, and in real terms the victim is indeed helpless and thereby vulnerable; but on another level they cease to be in contact with the experience. The sense of self as intact goes, and is replaced by a sense of being there whilst not being there; of knowing what is occurring and not knowing – an example is of a child being abused who experiences himself as floating on the ceiling watching the abuse take place on the bed below. He sees the abuse; he recognizes the victim as himself, but he does not feel the pain, and he does not at that point connect it with the self.

A further distinction between dissociation and repression is that:

> Whereas the discernment of repression involves an inference – that a piece of conscious mental life gives disguised expression to a feeling, impulse or perception that is unacceptable to the conscious mind – dissociation is directly observable. Dissociation is observable either by the therapist who perceives the patient switching into different states of mind, or by the patient who reports dissociative experiences such as depersonalisation ... repression, by contrast, is not directly observed or experienced and is not in itself a symptom: there are no 'repressive disorders' listed in the DSM. (Mollon, 1999: 65)

Many survivors of childhood sexual and physical abuse develop some kind of dissociative ability. When the child is overwhelmed by the abuse, dissociation isolates the catastrophic experience and allows the central self to escape from pain and reality. Essentially the self alters and detaches. Conflicts are shelved that would be present if this dissociation had not occurred, for example between loving and hating, and needing and fearing the important but abusing object. There is no resolution; instead there is a disowning of the conflict. It therefore affects the sense of unity of self and thereby creates disturbance in many aspects of memory and identity.

An interesting question is why does dissociation take place and not repression. This is a complex issue and there is no simple answer. It may be that repression fails under the impact, or has not been well enough established to withstand the assault. The age of the child under attack may also be significant, as may be their relationship with the abuser: if this is a primary attachment figure or someone on whom the child deeply depends this may increase the psychological need to dissociate: the younger they are the greater will be this need. Dissociation does have the psychological advantage of helping the child remain in contact with the attachment figure whilst losing contact with the effects of the trauma. Midgely, in his discussion of the reasons why some children have the capacity to dissociate, notes that:

> A more promising line of thought, one which has emerged in the last few years, is that certain types of attachment pattern in early childhood, especially the more recently recognised 'disorganised/disoriented' attachment pattern may predispose a child to dissociative defences when faced with abusive or traumatic experiences later in life. (Midgely, 2002: 41)

It should also be noted that there are many levels to dissociation: it is not one entity, or one presentation. Van der Kolk et al. (1996) suggest one method of describing these, noting that they are all essentially responses to trauma. They identify primary, secondary and tertiary dissociation. Primary occurs immediately in response to extreme trauma, for instance war, and involves somatosensory fragmentation; secondary is marked by the experiencing and observing self becoming separated; and tertiary, a response to repeated trauma over a long period of time, leads to what we know as multiple personality.

However, a broader description may be more enlightening in capturing the span of dissociation including those aspects that are helpful or pleasant and are present in the normal course of life. Examples of this are: day-dreaming; becoming absorbed; being lost in thought; 'drifting off' temporarily; the state between waking and sleeping; experiencing deep relaxation, and the ability temporarily and effectively to imagine yourself somewhere else when at the dentist or during uncomfortable medical examinations. Another level is a temporary response to a recent and identifiable stress or shock – an accident or bereavement, or a break-up of a relationship. Dissociative responses are frequently in evidence, and can be described as 'going on automatic pilot'; feeling numb; responding without feeling; experiencing a sense of non-reality, and feeling as if in a dream or in a daze. There can be a lack of awareness or recall of actions. Time and senses can be distorted or disrupted; there can be sleep disturbance, and the waking/sleeping divide might not be clear. These tend to be temporary or short-lived responses which decline as the experience becomes more incorporated into the self and the shock begins to lessen.

Another level can be present in adults as a result of ongoing trauma in childhood where splits in the self are apparent; for instance, a client who talks about 'a little girl me'; 'a bit of me that has to destroy everything I achieve'; 'a me that gets very nasty to other people sometimes'; 'a part of me that really wants to move on'; or 'a bit of me that gets drawn to violent men'. There is a sense of an internal battlefield but an awareness that these are parts of the whole, albeit in an uncomfortable fit. But the splits have not become autonomous selves.

In adults, as a response to ongoing trauma in childhood and often stemming from childhood, another layer of dissociation can be present. Some clients report out-of-body experiences, like the example of looking down on their self; or unconsciously entering or becoming an object; or becoming absorbed into/by the surrounding environment; or feeling no pain when ill or attacked and experiencing time distortions to a considerable degree (for example, 'losing' time) and space distortions. Essentially, there is a considerable degree of splitting of mind and body, and/or of feeling and event. As noted in the question on multiple personality (3.4) the most extreme end of this continuum is multiple personality – dissociative identity disorder – a response to extreme, ongoing, often bizarre abuse where autonomous, separate personalities develop from the splits.

Dissociative behaviour can occur in a session or be reported as happening in other situations. Although for the abused child it is a mechanism for avoiding or removing the self from the pain and fear, for the adult it can prevent normal functioning and relating, and can limit life experiences. It is potentially dangerous if time is lost and there is no knowledge of events during that time. Such dissociation is variously identifiable when it occurs in sessions. The client may go blank, fall silent, tail off in mid-sentence, lose the sense of the thread of communication, or forget what has been said; there may be a change in tone, voice, or demeanour and a strange feeling that the client is absent; the therapist can see they are there, but there is no sense of a real presence – rather a distance, a sense of unreality and lack of connectedness.

If this happens regularly, it is worth asking if there is a pattern to such occurrences. Are there any external or internal triggers that can be traced? Are there particular areas of discussion that cannot be tolerated but may not be recognized? Are there any objects in the counselling room that remind the client of abusive scenarios? Does it happen only when the chairs are in a certain position? Is the therapist triggering this response by something in their manner, whether it is either perceived transferentially by the client or is real? Therapists need to be very aware of their own process and countertransference: how they are feeling and reacting; what is happening to them in the relationship. If unsure whether the client is dissociated it may be possible to check this out: to ask if the client can pause and consider with the therapist what has happened: 'Can we try to understand what's happening together?' The counsellor needs to be sure that it is comfortable for the client to do this, remembering and acknowledging that dissociation is a deeply defensive manoeuvre arising originally from enormous fear and threat. Often, returning to the trigger can recreate in the client the very feelings or experience they at some level wished to avoid, so this is not a comfortable place for them to be.

The therapist can invite the client, if the client is able, to stay with the feeling; to try to recognize the trigger, and what it has recreated or reminded them of. It is important to remember that this defence has been a way of coping with huge anxiety and pain, so therapeutically the aim is to diminish the fear, by making it different, by finding a new way of coping, and by offering reassurance within a trusting and safe environment and relationship. Dissociating may be an avoidance of material the client does not yet feel able to explore but that is nevertheless seeping through, but that needs exploring.

Again, it is important to recognize that it may be that the counsellor's own style is unhelpful, or that the client is projecting on to the counsellor some aspects of the abusive experience that is then preventing further exploration. It feels unsafe. If triggers and defences can be identified and fears acknowledged, this opens the door for past abusive experiences to be looked at more safely, without repeating them. When the abuse was occurring there was noone there to help, so the counsellor's presence needs to be containing. Even acknowledging the client's need to distance themselves psychologically can begin to alter the pattern: the therapist is attentive, takes notice, takes the client seriously, and checks with the client how he or she can best help. As always, timing and pacing is of the essence: there is no room for impatience or for a therapist who needs to 'know' or be certain. It is essential to stay with what cannot be said, and cannot be tolerated as well as the muddle of not knowing. Patience, resilience, and presence, even when the client finds it so hard to be present themselves, are crucial.

* * *

3.4 Would I know when one of my clients was exhibiting signs of multiple personality disorder? And how should I then work with the client?

Multiple personality (or dissociative identity disorder (MPD/DID) as it is now more often referred to) is at a most extreme point on the continuum of dissociation and splitting. In my experience it is caused by extreme, repeated and often sustained attacks on a child, over a period of years, that are experienced as life-threatening by that child. This is likely to be in a context where at least one of the perpetrators (and there may be many) is the person the child most closely depends upon; in a situation where there is no possibility of literal escape, only psychological escape; where the child has been forced not to tell; and in a situation in which reality and non-reality are often strangely merged. The personalities that result take on a life and being of their own; they are distinct, may be amnesic of the others; they carry memories and experiences and have their own characteristics and ways of being. It is an extremely complex and clever defence mechanism arising from a child potentially being so overwhelmed by unmanageable pain and distress that in order to survive the experience has to be split up, taken up and contained by different selves.

The DSM-IV criteria for MPD/DID are:

- the presence of two or more distinct identities or personality states
- at least two of these identities or personality states recurrently take control of the person's behaviour
- inability to recall important information that is too extensive to be explained by ordinary forgetfulness
- not due to the direct effects of a substance or a general medical condition.

In counselling and therapy, multiple personality is not always obvious. Those who are multiple have often suffered psychiatric misdiagnosis in adulthood; their childhood history is usually one of systematic, ongoing and horrific abuse, and they have often experienced being labelled as liars. This can be in stark contrast to their abusers, who can hold trusted positions in society – disbelief is not a problem for them and they are not called liars. So given that trust is an issue for any abuse survivor, this is particularly stark for those with multiple personalities. Indicators of it include amnesic periods – inability to remember periods of time or life events; considerable doubt about what is real and not real; forgetting what a previous session was about; forgetting to come to sessions (in both these instances it could be because another personality was present); or self-presentation that varies in an extreme manner from session to session (clothes, hair style, mannerisms, tone of voice and vocabulary, likes and dislikes, level of self-confidence, content, can all be at remarkable variance). Signs such as these may indicate different selves being present at different sessions.

People who are multiple often present with turbulent experiences, with conflicting stories about the same event, claiming that both this and that happened; or the client reports, or is reported as, lying about their behaviour. They are constantly accused of being liars, and there is considerable confusion about events surrounding them. It can feel chaotic, confusing, controlling and contradictory to both the client and the counsellor. In some sessions clients may 'switch' between personalities, and there can be a very strange sense of suddenly being with a different person. If the therapist responds to this change the client may be able to acknowledge what has occurred:

> A moment or two later I was startled by her suddenly asking in a slightly different and rather aggressive voice: 'Got any paracetamol?' I replied that I did not have any and asked why she wanted them. She said she wanted to take an overdose and kill herself. I asked what had happened to the person I had just been speaking to who had felt more cheerful. 'She's gone,' was the reply. (Mollon, 1996: 109)

It is necessary to understand multiple personality as an unconscious defence mechanism, developed in the most extreme circumstances that most people could not imagine, and if described would prefer not to believe. For many people, multiple personality is beyond belief, but so are the experiences that lie behind it – except, tragically, they are true. It is also essential to understand 'someone with multiple personality experiences [as] having many different voices within. Each voice belongs to a separate autonomous personality with its own thoughts, feelings, emotion and memories' (Antony Black, 2000: 109); and that 'the person has a variety of alters [i.e. personalities] who serve different functions and who may cooperate or be in competition with one another' (Mollon, 1996: 108). Given that the personalities may or may not be aware of one another (some are and some are not) and that they can be of different ages, hold different memories, and may even have different views on being in therapy, it becomes clear that the therapeutic picture is inevitably complex and requires exceedingly careful work. The counsellor needs to recognize that essentially within one body there is a group of individual personalities, and that this is and has been an effective and creative defence mechanism.

Although multiple personality and dissociative conditions are nowadays a contentious issue, the issue is not new: there has been a serious and divided debate for a century. Particular studies, by Putman (1989) and Ross (1989) in the United States and Mollon (1996) in Britain, have been very significant in exploring and understanding the development of multiple personality as traumatogenic – that is, it arises as a response to severe child-hood abuse. At the same time other writers and practitioners have spoken in opposition. Essentially they (Aldridge-Morris (1989) in Britain; Hacking (1995) and Spanos (1996) in the United States) argue from an iatrogenic viewpoint: that is, they argue that multiple personalities are created by therapists who actively make suggestions, who may introduce reading material to further support their diagnosis, in combination with a client who is suggestible and compliant The patient is essentially understood as accommodating to a very particular and strongly held view of their ther-apist; so that the emergence of different personalities is an iatrogenic artefact. This stance assumes a very persuasively convincing and somewhat aggressive style on the part of the therapist, who enters the work with a clear idea of what is wrong. Those who oppose the iatrogenic viewpoint emphasize that therapists in general do not search for histories of abuse or for evidence of multiple personality, and in fact tend to defend against see-ing and hearing awful histories of abuse.

In working with multiple personality it is necessary to be aware of the controversy and these conflicting views, of the strength of the feelings expressed, and of the potential impact of all this on the client, the counsel-lor and the therapeutic alliance. Many find that their counselling or therapy training has not prepared them for such a complex and demanding pres-entation, and it can be difficult to find supervisors with sufficient experience. Seeking specialist help both for the therapist, or as a referral for the client can be appropriate and, as always, it is crucial to work within the limits of one's own expertise and knowledge. Those with MPD are extreme-ly vulnerable, and also individuals with MPD vary enormously: 'Although MPD patients have much in common with each other, they are also quite idiosyncratic, with their own complex internal structures and nuances of inner experiences. The idea of a standardised therapy for patients with MPD/DID seems a contradiction in terms' (Mollon, 1996: 140).

However complex and demanding the work is for the counsellor or ther-apist, there is a first time for working with any presentation, but in this particular instance I urge enormous care. Proceeding slowly and carefully is crucial, in the context of sufficient support and supervision. Boundaries need to be maintained, although within these the client needs appropriate control over the process, particularly in terms of speed and content of material presented. Deciding where to sit, sometimes having a shorter ses-sion if that is all that can be tolerated, and similarly missing a session, are all needs that may have to be accommodated. The therapist needs to con-tinually learn about the needs of the client from the client – the most careful and respectful attention has to be paid. Because it can seem chaot-ic the therapist has to resist any urge to take control: rarely is the ability to tolerate not knowing more needed. The internal struggle of those with multiple personalities is huge, and progress can be slow. Patience and fortitude are required, as is the ability to sit it out when nothing seems to be happening. Work with multiple personality always has to be undertaken within a therapeutic context that is and remains continually aware of the depth and extent of the trauma that created it:

> Those with multiple personality have to learn about very difficult events ... the ordeal of discovering the abuse they have survived may be tremendous and especially traumatic for the host personality, who may have no recollection of anything but a loving and secure background. (Walker, 1992: 136)

I have noted that boundaries are crucial in abuse work, but in this instance they may need to be differently drawn to those applicable and appropriate to more usual therapeutic situations. It is the therapist's job to hold boundaries, but also to review their ongoing value in terms of what is being presented: there are occasions when they have to be shifted and adapted, as does the range of therapeutic interventions. Different ways of communicating with different selves may be needed, including painting, drawing, writing, using work books, tape recorders and keeping journals. Offering a range of various therapeutic styles for different selves reflects how other therapists may work with different types of client: it is a more flexible and extended model. This should always be done with care and forethought, not as a response to disillusion or desperation, but as a considered therapeutic plan.

Time and timing create significant boundary questions. Some of the personalities may belong to very frightened children, so that careful attention has to be paid to ensure that it is an adult who leaves the room at the end of a session. It may be necessary to prolong a session, or ensure that a safe place and person is available, if a distressed child is present who will not be safe in the wider world. This is not boundary breaking, but having a different concept of boundaries, which remain crucial to maintaining the safety of counselling for client and counsellor. A real therapeutic difficulty can arise if a pattern emerges of such a child personality entering the session shortly before it is due to end. Although there are potentially many explanations for such a pattern, and this can be explored with the client, as can strategies for responding, it may be that the child personality needs to be given time earlier in the session. If this is done she will then rest contented or can be asked (as a real child can be) to give someone else some time. It may be that the child represents an aspect of the abusive experience in which she could never express her need for help.

It is evident that time can be a very real and difficult issue in this work; this is further intensified by the possibility that different personalities can compete for time and react physically and psychologically against how much time each one has. Other therapeutic issues arise – for example, dealing with conflicts over power with and between the different selves. They can compete with each other, fearing that another will gain complete control. Controlling personalities can be in evidence, taking the role of silencing everyone; destructive personalities can believe that they are to blame, feel dirty and may self-harm. Other selves know what happened in the past and have the role of hiding the memories. These different selves have different needs, so that an apparently appropriate therapeutic response that may be helpful to one personality can be infuriating or confounding to another. Transference is similarly complex and multi-faceted: many selves can be involved and may therefore produce a variety of transferential responses.

In working with clients with this presentation one aim might be for the personalities to become integrated. However, for some people with multiple personality this is neither desired nor perceived as possible – the different personalities are polarized to such an extent that this is rendered impossible. The therapeutic aim is rather to produce a system that is more collaborative and less hidden; and where a degree of awareness and knowledge makes life more comfortable and less destructive. For other clients the process of integration is possible and desired; it involves a long therapeutic process of working through the needs of the various personalities, requiring a strong therapeutic alliance with each. With others, integration appears to be a more natural and spontaneous process that occurs gradually as the need for such powerful dissociation recedes. Whatever the resolution, be it integration or an increased collaboration, the difficulties for those with multiple personality do not neatly end there. Learning to live without dissociation can be experienced as profoundly painful, since new coping mechanisms that do not involve such profound distancing have to be discovered and experienced.

* * *

3.5 Last week one of my clients began to shake and cower in her chair as she vividly recalled, almost as if it were happening now, how her abuser touched her. I am not sure I handled it very well, although I tried to be empathic to how frightened she was. Was she experiencing a flashback? Could I have responded better?

This certainly sounds like a flashback. A flashback is a particularly complex manifestation of dissociation, an uninvited and apparently unconscious action replay of a disturbing and traumatic event over which the person has little control. It is a very powerful re-experiencing that is quite different to other forms of recall, however painful they too can be. The survivor is often totally back in the experience, reliving it, and feeling what she felt then, emotionally and physically. Extremes of fear and panic can be present, as can physical pain and discomfort. Other flashbacks are less extreme, so awareness of the real and current situation is variable. Some become lost in the flashback and therefore cannot explore it at the time: they can only experience and feel it; whereas others have some awareness that it is a flashback and yet that they are also present in the here-and-now. Whatever point it may be in this continuum, it is an unwelcome and frightening intrusion: the past becomes the present and becomes re-enacted.

Flashbacks often occur as clients begin to deal with the abuse – they can follow on disclosures. Some survivors experience large numbers of flash-backs, and as one is dealt with it is replaced by another. Flashbacks can be momentary, or they can last some time. But they will end naturally, although sometimes the client can be helped to come back, depending on their degree of awareness. On occasion all that is possible is to sit it out with the client and wait for it to end. During the flashback, if the client is very 'lost' or very regressed (especially to a pre-verbal stage), the first pri-ority is to keep them safe as non-intrusively as possible; otherwise there is a real danger of some aspects of the abusive experience being repeated. Particular caution must be exercised at this point over touching or holding the client. This may be necessary if it is the only way to keep the client safe, although this can sometimes be managed by ensuring the survivor is not, for instance, near a wall where they can hurt their head, and that any objects that could be harmful are moved. Holding or touching a client dur-ing a flashback may lessen the terror, but equally may increase it if it is experienced in any way as abusive.

During the flashback it is crucial for the counsellor to remain calm and grounded. This is difficult, as it can be almost as frightening to observe a flashback as to experience it; and this is especially so the first time one is encountered. It can help the client, and may help the counsellor to feel they can do something, to quietly reassure even if it appears the client can-not hear you. It can be helpful to repeat that the experience itself was then and is not now, that now the client is safe, and that you will ensure their safety until they are ready to regain adult control. Calling the client by name, reminding them who the therapist is, and where they are, can also assist them in returning to the present.

A client who had a flashback of being abused as a toddler remained in that state for about 40 minutes. She was able to say afterwards that as time went on my voice began to be audible. She began to note the tone and sense it as reassuring. Gradually she began to decipher words and then to make sense of what I was saying. It is hard to know whether this helped her through this any quicker but it did seem to offer her some comfort as she returned. It is important not to shout, even if the client is making so much noise that the counsellor imagines she is not being heard; and to avoid any language which could be construed as aggressive or demanding, for instance, 'Look at me'; 'Listen to me', as this type of language is often used by abusers during the abuse.

If it is possible for the client to do so, and this depends on their degree of immersion in the flashback, the therapist can encourage her or him to say what she is experiencing. The therapist needs to listen carefully because the flashback is itself narrating an aspect of the trauma that is unresolved and needs exploration and examination. Because the client is to some degree unavailable and inaccessible during the flashback; much of the work is done when it is over. Then, with help, she may be able to locate the trigger: whether it was a sound, smell, certain words, seeing a person who is reminiscent of the abuser, the touch of a certain fabric – such potential triggers are numerous and vary from survivor to survivor. It is not always possible to locate triggers immediately, but it often is with time. Encouraging the client to be more in touch by monitoring what is happening can help them begin to feel more in control.

Working with the client on the content of the flashback and its associations so that this is made more familiar; and working with and through the associated feelings helps to lessen the intensity of the original experience. Once experiences and memories are consciously worked with, validated, and acknowledged without the counsellor being overwhelmed, the unconscious need to 'flood' by flashback declines. As I write elsewhere, 'the terrifying secrets that are often recalled in flashbacks start to lose their power when the private is made public' (Walker, 1992: 180). As with other traumas, the events experienced in the flashback may need to be worked through time and time again before their power recedes. It can help the client to go through the original incident, but working on different endings with the aim of normalizing, controlling and regaining power. A young woman experienced a flashback of the sexual abuse by her cousin when she was five every time she attempted to have sex with her partner, and she visualized this experience in counselling over a period of time. It terrified her at first but she reached a point where she visualized her 5-year-old self taking on her current age and size, and saw herself pushing the abuser out of the window. She described in graphic detail his crushed body, which was reminiscent of how she had felt crushed by him. Not only did this begin to prevent the flashback, but it also gave access in the counselling to her feelings of rage, which had previously not been acknowledged as she had found them too frightening to explore. If flashbacks, as in this example, occur during sexual activity the client may need encouragement to share with her partner the experience and work out strategies together.

Explaining to the client what a flashback is so that it becomes comprehensible is an important part of the process. People often fear they are going mad, particularly if they have experienced prior unhelpful responses, sadly not unusual. Making sense of what is occurring, and recognizing it as an understandable and common response to trauma can be very reassuring. The client can also learn cognitive 'grounding' techniques to reduce the likelihood and the intensity of flashbacks, and partners and friends can help with these once learnt. It has been noted (Simonds, 1994) that during a flashback the intensity of the dissociative experience is increased by a tendency to withdraw from the immediate environment; for example, the survivor often curls up, is unable to make eye contact and draws in upon herself. Helping the survivor to place their feet firmly on the floor; to grasp the arms of the chair, to say who they are and what they do, or to talk of plans for their week, can all be helpful procedures. In time, as the client herself begins to recognize triggers to flashbacks, these techniques in conjunction with that recognition can prevent them occurring, or can lessen their intensity. The overall aim is not to suppress flashbacks or disturbing memories, but to work with the client as they are experienced. Helping them to process these is a necessary step in coming to terms with their abusive experiences, as well as assisting the client in moving beyond these.

After a flashback the client can be left feeling exhausted, shaking and drained. It is important to encourage self-care at this time:

> After experiencing a flashback and discussing it with her helper, a woman should be encouraged to look after herself as if she has had a recent injury. This could involve going to bed, having a warm bath, taking mild pain-killers, but most of all giving herself permission to comfort and take care of herself. For many incest survivors, this is a totally new experience and can lead to better self care. (Hall and Lloyd, 1989:125)

To sum up: it is essential to stay calm, to reassure, to wait patiently, and to understand what is going on. Additionally, if working in an agency, it is crucial to prevent anyone else acting in an unhelpful way out of panic, personal inability to cope, or through lack of knowledge. The experience of flashbacks can be a noisy and deeply disturbing one for all concerned, so it is important that agencies and those that work in them have the necessary skill base to contain the client at these times.

* * *

3.6 I have clients from time to time who self-harm, and I have noticed that these are sometimes people who recall physical or sexual abuse. Is there a link? And how should I respond to clients who either tell me, or show me clear signs, of self-harm?

Self-harm is manifested in many ways. It can be by the person injuring themselves through overdosing, cutting, burning, biting, excessive drinking or drug use; or harming themselves by failure to care for the self, not eating or over-eating, by creating circumstances where accidents are more likely to happen, by not allowing or destroying good things, or staying in bad situations, for example destructive relationships. Other methods of self-harming occur through too much or inappropriate exercise or intentionally depriving oneself of sleep. Injuring the self often starts during childhood, although may not be recognized as such; others who self-injure only begin in adolescence or adulthood. Self-injury is closely linked to abuse in childhood (de Young, 1982; van der Volk et al., 1991): de Young finds that in her sample of incest victims more than 50 per cent had self-injured. As noted by Arnold and Babiker: 'Self injury is more common amongst women than men and this difference is likely to reflect the different pressures and expectations placed on men and women in our society. Where men self injure, it is usually when they have less power than is usual for men' (1998: 134).

In childhood, self-harm can start as an attempt by the child to protect themselves from the abuser by making themselves unattractive, or as an expression of self-disgust and shame or anger, or as a response to having no other power. For some children and adults it is a response to extreme dissociation triggered by the abuse. Self-harm can be a way for the child and the adult to end the dissociative experience, to rejoin the body to the self, and of ensuring that she or he knows that they are still alive. Herman comments: 'Abused children discover at some point that the feeling can be most effectively terminated by a major jolt to the body. The most dramatic method of achieving this result is through the deliberate infliction of injury' (Herman, 1992: 110). Children who self-harm may also be expressing despair, or attempting to communicate that something is very wrong. In addition, physically abused children often associate pain with love, and self-injury can paradoxically be comforting and reassuring.

Self-injury is thus multi-faceted, with many different meanings for different people. In adult survivors who self-injure the factors described that apply to abused children similarly apply. In addition, abuse makes intimate adult relationships, or sometimes any relationships, difficult. Ordinary interpersonal conflicts may produce intense anxiety, depression or rage, and the survivor may be without the verbal or social skills to respond appropriately. Abuse in childhood does not provide any model of containment of difficult feelings, so self-harm can be a response to such feelings. This is particularly likely if injury comes to be associated with finding temporary relief. It is important to note that injury can provide a real sense of relief, because pain is not actually felt at the time; instead there is a welcome release from the pressure and pain felt inside. Cutting in particular, and watching the flow of blood, can be experienced as cathartic.

For others an intense sense of badness and low self-esteem resulting from the childhood abuse is associated with the pain inflicted by others. In turn this can lead to the infliction of pain on the self as a punishment for the badness they feel is deeply within them. A desperate need can lead to self-harm; a need to communicate felt distress; to speak in actions when words are not available or are not sufficient. So self-harm can be an expression of feeling, or an avoiding of feelings; a desire to inflict pain or a way of expressing pain or a method of avoiding pain. It can also be a desperate cry for help. Some survivors of abuse experience deep internal conflicts, and self-injury can represent an internal battle between a destructive self and a more self protective self: at the point of self-harming the former is winning.

Whilst a response and reaction from others may be wanted by cutting in visible places and making the wounds very apparent, this is not always so. Injuries may be carried out secretly, in private, according to rituals, and the resulting wounds are well hidden. However, at some level, all those who self-harm are likely to be searching consciously or unconsciously for comfort, nurturing and acknowledgement from others.

Frequently derogatory labels are attached to those who self-harm. They are called attention seeking, difficult, demanding, manipulative, aggressive or dangerous. Such labels tend to diminish the person and their actions, and consequently self-harm is either not taken seriously enough or is responded to punitively. An example of this was described by an 18-year-old after she had cut herself sufficiently badly to need stitches. This was done without anaesthetic, on the basis that she had already cut herself, and intentionally inflicted pain, and that she could and should therefore tolerate being stitched without pain relief.

It should be noted that self-injury should not be confused with suicidal behaviour – it has a different origin and serves a different purpose. Self-injury is not intended to kill, and many of those survivors who harm themselves see it as a way of self-preservation and of preventing suicide by ridding themselves of some of the unbearable feelings or tension. It has, however, to be recognized that in this respect self-harming can go wrong and more serious damage can be done than was intended.

In working with someone who self-harms, it must be taken seriously, but without panicking or over-reacting. Sometimes counsellors fail to hear or acknowledge what they see, as if in their desire not to overreact they fail to react at all. Some feel that if they pay too much attention to it, it will encourage the survivor to further self-harm, but this attitude fails to understand the meaning of the act. But it can be true that 'in the short term, counselling or therapy may lead to an increase in self-injury as the individual faces up to buried experiences and feelings' (Arnold and Babiker, 1998: 144). It is important to check out how serious the self-harm is and if it is likely to be life-threatening, even if generally most self-harm is not.

Beginning to communicate with the client itself starts the process of offering another model of dealing with difficulties: they can be expressed and verbalized, and managed and contained by another person (and ultimately by the survivor). It is the first step in finding a way to help the client to listen to themselves and see what is happening to them, and so find other ways of coping. If self-harm has become habitual the triggers and sources to this may have become very lost: there is no wedge between the feeling and the act. Beginning to track back to the client's internal experience prior to the self-harming, and how they feel afterwards, can help to recover a more conscious awareness of what caused the self-harm.

It can be illuminating to explore with the client whether or not he or she is aware that hurting themselves is a way of speaking without words. It may be the first time it has been conceptualized in this way with them: that in itself harm is an attempt to say something that previously there was no other way of communicating. It invites exploration of whether there might be other ways of expressing themselves now. This has to be when the client is ready. The counsellor needs to be careful over issues of power and control. It does not help to ask someone, or tell them to stop hurting themselves, whereas acknowledging that self-harm has had a very important purpose, and is therefore hard to give up, is an important communication of understanding.

It is also helpful to check out with the client how they feel about talking about the self-harm, and provide space for them to say how they understand it, and what it might mean. Clients may feel ambivalent about other ways of coping, remembering that self-harm can be comforting and protective, or that the anger they feel is so great that this feels the only safe way to express it. Recognizing and working with ambivalence, and with the split between the part of the self that might want to stop and other parts that oppose it, is a key part of the process.

It is also important to work with clients to help them recognize and tolerate uncomfortable feelings, learning that these need not destroy them now, whilst acknowledging that when they were small it may have felt like that. Clients may need to be assured that self-harm is an understandable response to awful things happening; but that it is possible to change – albeit it may be a struggle, and that others have experienced the same.

Counsellors themselves may have strong feelings about self-harm. They may find it abhorrent and difficult to hear of the wounds inflicted, and actually seeing the damage to the body can be very distressing. It is important for counsellors to deal with and contain their own feelings, if they are to be containing to the client. Being reasonably matter of fact in discussing self-harm helps in putting it and keeping it on the agenda of subjects to be explored. Exploring practical possibilities helps some clients, although only if their ambivalence has been addressed reasonably successfully. Helping clients identify their own danger zones (for examples, knives), or danger times (like having contact with the abuser), and exploring alternative strategies can be empowering.

Essentially the counsellor is helping the client to fully recognize the nature of their self-harm, by placing it in the wider context of understanding it, and the reasons for it, both unconscious and conscious. It is crucial to recognize that it is not a simple presentation of self; it means different things to different people, and even within the same person the meaning can be variable. Recognizing that it can serve many functions for the one person has to be one starting point. Another is the creation of a containing relationship. In these ways it becomes possible to begin the process of helping the client to find other ways of managing strong and painful feelings.

* * *

3.7 I imagine it's not surprising that a client who has been abused finds sex distasteful, but the person I am working with wants very much to please her partner, who is becoming very wary of touching her. Should I try to concentrate on the sexual difficulties, perhaps even use some cognitive-behavioural methods? Or will her sexual response change as we work on the other issues she presents?

Sexual problems are a well-documented effect of childhood sexual abuse (Finkelhor, 1979; Herman, 1981; Jehu and Gazan, 1983), although in my clinical experience sexual difficulties can also arise from physical and emotional abuse. The link may not be so obvious, and research does suggest (Briere, 1992) that sexual difficulties are most often associated with sexual rather than with other abuse. Nevertheless it is important to be aware of this as a possibility and a reality for some. Whatever form the abuse takes it involves the child submitting to the will of another. Many learn very quickly that the abuse may be lessened, or at least got through more quickly, if they are compliant; and this in turn translates itself, often unconsciously, into adult sexual relationships.

I assume here that the writer of the question is referring to a client who has been sexually abused. The experience of the sexually abused child is an impossible one: they often trust the abuser, and the abuser has put considerable effort into gaining this trust. The perpetrator carefully grooms, brainwashes and emotionally coerces the child into believing it is either their fault, or that they enjoy it, or have invited it, or are in some other way responsible for the abuse. In addition, if the child's body responds pleasurably the knot tightens, further intensified by the child's fear as they respond to threats made by a powerful larger person. The child may also dissociate, or may quickly learn that compliance not only lessens the abuse, but may additionally lead to longed-for praise and comfort afterwards. It is an emotional nightmare that is difficult to comprehend, a nightmare that is particularly appalling when the abuser is a very close relative of the child. The viciousness of this, and its profound effects, are described horribly by Kluft in his recounting of what a pimp looks for in looking for young woman to become prostitutes:

> What is important above all is obedience. And how do you get obedience? You get obedience if you get women who have had sex with their fathers, their uncles, their brothers – you know, someone they love and fear to lose so that they do not dare to defy. Then you are nicer to the woman than they ever were, and more dangerous as well. They will do anything to keep you happy. (Kluft, 1990: 25)

In the situation described in this question the woman is anxious to please her husband, but he in turn is uncomfortable and recognizes that this is undesirable. He sounds as if he is feeling anxious and wary himself. In terms of a therapeutic response, several possibilities may be appropriate. Key to all of these is careful discussion and negotiation with the client; but were this my client I would be very aware of the possibility that she may want to please me too, particularly if she was in any way feeling that she was at fault in the counselling by not getting it right, or by not being good enough.

One possibility is to continue individual work that aims at building trust, and helps the client identify and explore the issues and patterns in her life. At the same time it is important to recognize that change will not occur quickly and that her defences will be strongly in place and cannot be dismantled quickly. Any approach must ensure that she does not experience any re-abuse. We do not know here how long counselling has been going on, or what approach the counsellor has been used. One obvious question is to ask whether the client wants to concentrate on her sexual difficulties? If this is an aspect of her life that is deeply troubling in an urgent and immediate way, particularly if she has a concern that her marriage is dangerously in crisis, then it would be utterly reasonable to focus on this.

The question remains how best to do this, and one model is to work with the couple. But this too is fraught with potential difficulty. In any event moving from an individual to a couple focus can be problematic. The individual client may feel he or she has lost 'their' counsellor; confidentiality is complex (for example, what can be shared with the partner and what cannot); and with an abused client there may be repetition of the abusive situation, whereby boundaries are moved and invaded, where saying no is not a real possibility to them. Another option is to refer her husband for his own counselling so that he has time and space to explore the impact on him of the current situation. Ultimately this may open up the possibility of couple work with the two counsellors. Using this last model, the dilemmas posed above may still exist, but can be rendered far more manageable. It is more straightforward to lay down clear boundaries and guidelines for that particular piece of therapeutic work.

In terms of offering a cognitive-behavioural approach focusing on the sexual difficulties the questioner does not say whether or not he or she is well qualified to do so. If not, this is not an area to dabble in, but if the client feels that such an approach would be helpful (and again false compliance, and fear of rejection, could be issues here) it may be appropriate to draw on the help of a colleague who is specifically skilled and trained in this approach. This could work alongside the existing counselling work, or the present counselling could be put on hold whilst the other sessions take place. If working alongside, great care needs to be taken to avoid potential splitting or simply creating confusion. Both practitioners would then need to be clear regarding their roles, and if the client permits should be in discussion with one another. Done well, such professional co-operation and clarity can be very helpful to an abused client: it models honesty, clarity, co-operation, taking the client seriously, and above all the ability of two people to work together holding appropriate boundaries in the interest of the client. This is the very antithesis of the parental model so often experienced by the abuse survivor.

Whatever decision is taken on therapeutic interventions at this stage, the counsellor needs to be very sure that he or she is not acting out their own frustrations that the work is difficult, and not progressing as he or she may wish. It is crucial to be able to stay firmly with difficulty and uncertainty in this work, but it is also important to know when the therapeutic interventions of one practitioner are insufficient, and so to think creatively and draw appropriately on the expertise of others. This should be done only after discussion in supervision and in consultation with the client.

CHAPTER 4
Therapeutic concerns

4.1. One client I am seeing is a Christian, and keeps talking about the need to forgive the man who abused her when she was a child. I find it difficult to think how anyone can forgive that sort of behaviour, and am not sure how to avoid treading on sensitive ground.

For counsellors faced with this issue there can be several dilemmas. One may be a desire to respect the religious beliefs of a client and not to be seen as questioning these. For a counsellor who shares these beliefs it is important not to become collusive and make assumptions. For both it is important that the question of faith, whilst being acknowledged and respected, does not prevent the exploration of what forgiveness means for this client and where her need to forgive comes from. For example, I have worked with survivors previously seen in counselling services operating in a religious context where the need to forgive is a central ethos. This is communicated to the client, rather than coming from them, whereas other similarly placed services do not operate within this agenda and help the client explore issues in their own terms. It may therefore be important to ascertain the source of this need – does it come from within or has it been imposed from without?

Forgiveness is not straightforward and can mean a myriad of different things. It has many implications and potential traps for both counsellor and client. Some survivors see forgiveness as the only way either to let go of the past and move on, or to resolve painful feelings; or if the abuser is someone they love, they see it as a way of holding on to the good parts whilst ridding themselves of the bad. For others, as is possible with this client, a perceived inability to forgive may clash with religious beliefs. It can also be a response to an abuser requesting forgiveness, sometimes as part of an apparent apology. In this instance there may be family pressure to forgive and forget, where failure by the survivor to do so can be viewed by the family as an attack, and an obstinate refusal to let bygones be bygones. For the survivor this is very guilt inducing, especially if they have previously been labelled as the difficult one in the family, as can happen with abuse victims. The pressure to forgive, and the guilt if this is not forthcoming is intensified when the abuser is elderly: comments such as 'You can't go on holding that against an old man'; 'It was years ago. Why can't you just let it go?' or 'Give him some peace before he goes; he's sorry and he never meant to hurt you' are not uncommonly expressed in a family where abuse has occurred.

Salter comments:

> When forgiveness is offered by the victim not so much for his or her own purposes but to appease others or to ameliorate the family situation, it may be counter-productive ... forgiving an offender because he wants or needs the forgiveness is even more harmful for the survivor. When is healing for the survivor ever about servicing the offender's needs? (Salter, 1995: 152)

It is crucial to explore with the client the context in which their desire for forgiveness takes place, the meaning it has for them, and their hopes regarding the outcome, for themselves and for others. As with confronting the abuser (see Question 2.5) it is helpful to take time with the client to explore whether such hopes and aims are realistic. It can be deeply disappointing to a survivor to find that, as with confrontation, forgiveness may not produce the solution they had expected. Carefully exploring the possibility that forgiveness may not be the only resolution can ease the pressure on the client. If forgiveness is regarded as a panacea and then fails, this can leave the survivor feeling that *they* have failed. Acknowledging with the survivor that what is important is that they move on from the abuse and achieve some resolution, and that forgiveness may be their route forward, but that other possibilities do exist, can open up other potential arenas for change.

Ultimately the need to forgive is a personal choice for the survivor. But it is important to recognize that the picture is often complicated by the needs of other family members, or the abuser themselves, and then does not become a matter of choice. Yet again, there is an imposition of the will of another, and abusive patterns are repeated as the survivor is made to act in a certain way. The same can be true of groups or individuals who are significant to the survivor, who insist on the need for forgiveness. It is clear from work with survivors that some genuinely feel a need to forgive, but it is equally clear that for others this is not the case. This latter group clearly state that they regard the abuse and the abuser as unforgivable, although it does not prevent them moving on and leaving the abusive experiences behind them; they simply feel that some acts committed by some people are not forgivable. Others say they have forgiven the person, although not what they did. There are many variations to this theme, but what is important within the counselling relationship is that there is sufficient trust and safety established to be able to explore forgiveness as another theme in the therapeutic process. What is not helpful is for it to become a no-go area because of the religious connotations referred to in this question. If it is important to the client that they forgive, it is likely to have a more positive outcome, as long as they reach an understanding of what this means for them, and this is a genuinely personal choice rather than one imposed either by religious rhetoric or by the narcissistic needs of an abuser.

Sgroi and Sargent suggest that 'forgiveness should not be viewed as the sine qua non of coming to terms with the relationship with the abuser' (1993: 31). Perhaps, as ever, the key is to hold the survivor's needs at the forefront of the work, recognizing that different people respond differently to their abusers in their journey forward.

* * *

4.2 How can I be sure that I do not re-traumatize my clients in counselling?

It is not easy for survivors to seek help: much of their childhood experience indicates that those whom society deems to be trustworthy are in reality not so. Counsellors need to show they are trustworthy and have to demonstrate that they will not be abusive. Survivors have to be offered good, effective, sensitive services if re-traumatizing is to be avoided. Short-term counselling (see Question 6.1), for example, has to be undertaken with particular caution and care if it is not to be experienced as invasive and overwhelming.

This is not to say that open-ended and long-term work is not without dangers either. It can promote an unhelpful over-dependence; a lack of therapeutic rigour in terms of monitoring its effectiveness, and the timeless quality that comes from lack of clarity about the ending can also resonate with the abusive experience. It is not just the question of what type of counselling is available, but also how it is available and how it is operated. Any theoretical approach is open to being over-rigidly used so that the client is made to fit the model rather than the model to fit the person. Very precise views on what helps can be held. For instance, some argue that for the client to recover they have to forgive their abuser (see Question 4.1); others feel the client must get to a point where they can talk about all the abuse; others that inner child work is always helpful and the key to resolution. Some argue that it is better to have a counsellor who has been abused because they really understand (see Question 5.1); or conversely that a counsellor who has been abused is essentially unhelpful because their agenda will always be in the way.

Perhaps what is most important is that the counsellor works with the client to identify their concerns and needs, rather than imposing a model.

Accounts from survivors provide some examples of apparent help actually repeating abusive experiences rather than alleviating them. One described filling in a pre-assessment questionnaire for health service psychotherapy. She was asked if she had experienced abuse as a child, followed by further questions. This was her experience:

> I wanted to say sod off and mind your own business – I'm not putting that on a form. But I was really worried they wouldn't take me on then, and I can't afford to pay. And if I lied and said no I'd be found out later, and ever since I was small I've been accused of lying. So I ticked 'yes' but didn't say more. I waited ages to be seen and then at the assessment she asked me to say more and I didn't want to. I wasn't going to see her again. It felt very abusive. It was a really bad start although the person I saw in the end was OK.

Such questioning imposes dilemmas for the survivor who is caught in a no-win situation. If they answer 'yes', they can feel invaded, angry, frightened and threatened. They do not know what happens to this information, either who sees it or what is done with it. This is particularly worrying for survivors who have been abused by people in the care professions. If they say 'no', they may fear retribution for lying, an accusation made to many abused children. For many it is not a simple question. Memories may be hazy and uncertain, or the survivor cannot yet define their experience, even to themselves, let alone to anonymous others via an even more anonymous piece of paper.

Another person who was offered help using a cognitive-behavioural approach commented that she was quite capable of thinking for herself how to behave and think differently, the problem was she felt something deep inside would never allow it. She had a strong sense, rightly or wrongly, that it had not been recognized that the approach was not right for her, and it was suggested that there was something the matter with her for not fitting it. This resonated with her childhood experience of always being blamed for the abuse. But approaches at the opposite end of the spectrum can be equally problematic for survivors when insensitively used. A psychodynamically trained counsellor in supervision told his supervisor of his client's anger towards him in a session. He felt this to be an example of negative transference – the client was responding to him as if he were her abusive father. Although in another situation this may have been accurate, it was not so in this instance. The counsellor had made a mistake and the client was appropriately angry. If this had not been identified in supervision the client would have again experienced a situation where reality was denied and reframed, just as had happened to her as a child. As it was, in the next session the counsellor acknowledged his mistake and apologized for it. This was enormously significant to his client, representing an important step forward for her and their relationship, and an important learning point for him.

Another example comes from a survivor who at her initial assessment had hesitantly made clear that she could work only with a woman therapist. Eighteen months later she received an appointment with a male therapist. Again, she felt unheard and not taken seriously. She attended three sessions but could not continue. In her first session she was overcome with terror. She could not speak. For half an hour she said nothing, and neither did the therapist. Her fear grew. His presence became ever more threatening and she experienced a flashback to the abuse, which itself had taken place in silence. After half an hour he commented on the silence and interpreted it as resistance. She attempted to explain what was happening and could not. After session three, in which she had tried both to challenge her therapist and to explain her difficulty, in neither case successfully, she gave up. She wrote to the therapist who had assessed her, explaining and asking for an appointment with a woman. The reply was that she must work on her difficulties with the therapist, and that she could not be offered another. She did not go back. What followed was horribly similar to earlier childhood events: she alternated between being withdrawn and explosively angry. She felt once again that she had been damaged and betrayed, not listened to, not taken seriously, in yet another situation where she had no power and no real voice. Nothing was resolved. Another layer of pain was added, only in turn to be repressed. She would not risk seeing other counsellors or therapists, because the chance of further hurt was just too great.

There are other factors that counsellors need to take into account in order to reduce the risk of repeating abusive patterns. Policies regarding confidentiality need to be carefully established; and the client should have accurate and clear information relating to these. The client need to feels she or he is being taken seriously and believed. Careful, empathic and attentive listening is vital to the process, really attempting to understand what the client is saying. Assurance needs to be provided that the client may proceed at their own pace; that they will not be pushed into revealing detail that they are not ready to talk about, but that when they are ready to disclose more (see Question 1.3), the counsellor will listen, will not be shocked or overwhelmed, and will support them.

It is crucial to be aware of the misuse of power in the adult's own childhood and not to misuse the power implicit in the counselling situation. One way to achieve this is to allow the client to control the pace and development of counselling sessions. Being particularly aware of boundary issues is also central, remembering that all abused children have had their boundaries invaded. Therapists need to be very clear about their own boundaries, never offering more than they can realistically give. Runa Wolf, an abuse survivor who gives a moving and at times horrifying account of various unhelpful encounters with doctors, mental health professionals and counsellors, puts this very well when describing how she at last had a positive experience:

> I would describe the therapists stance as one of *presence* combined with an impeccable sense of her own *boundaries* and absolute respect for my *autonomy*. This cluster of qualities allows us to have a therapeutic partnership where the therapist is fully available *in the service of my therapy*. Treated with such clarity and respect, I have been able to work at my own pace, and to set my own limits, thus creating some healthy boundaries of my own. (Wolf, 1998: 25, original italics)

As noted in 1.4, abused clients can be particularly affected by the position of their chair. They may be particularly disturbed by interruptions in the session, or by a change of room or time over which they have no control. The counsellor needs to be sensitive to these issues and take them seriously. If sessions are interrupted or disrupted it should not be ignored, but acknowledged and worked with. Perhaps what is key is an awareness in the counsellor of the possibility of their approach re-traumatizing the individual client. This can be a surprisingly hard recognition and acknowledgement. Most practitioners would honestly declare and believe that this would absolutely never be either their intention or their wish. Similarly, those training counsellors would make the same declaration. And yet it is clear that the client's experience does not always match the counsellor's perception of themselves. I have noted already that certain approaches can be experienced as invasive: for example, detailed history-taking and questionnaire use. Therapists need to ask themselves questions such as: Who is this for? Is this necessary? Is the timing appropriate? Is it really helpful? Care should be taken not to ask too many questions, while explanations about why information is being requested can lessen anxiety. As the earlier example demonstrates, for some clients their own choice of the gender of their counsellor is absolutely crucial.

The style of counselling is important. Interpretations, even if technically accurate, may be experienced as being invasive, or suggest that the counsellor has magical powers: remember that abusers often imbued themselves with such powers. Clever interpretations can place the counsellor in a similar category of magical and mysterious knowledge. Similarly, approaches that set homework tasks can be deeply anxiety-provoking for the survivor if they do not wish to undertake them, or feel unable to. Tasks may trigger memories or experiences that the survivor is not ready to explore or face, yet it can be hard to say no.

Many survivors speak very warmly of their experience of counselling and it should be stressed that all theoretical models can facilitate good and helpful therapeutic work as well as be misused. Perhaps the counsellors who work best with abuse survivors are those who, whatever their training and their theoretical base, are comfortable in being flexible, continually monitor themselves and the process, always think what will work best for the particular person, and are able to manage uncertainty. Additionally it is crucial that counsellors, while always working towards increasing their knowledge and skill base, are constantly aware of the limitations of their knowledge, and of the mistakes in the past that have been made on the basis of unproven myths and misconceptions. No doubt this is a complex set of skills and qualities: sufficient confidence to work with survivors, a firm belief in one's ability, balanced by a humility and a modesty that does not believe in easy answers or formulaic responses.

* * *

4.3 As a male therapist, I am aware that I may not be picking up, or I am not having shared with me, information about sexual abuse. I seem to have fewer instances of this amongst my clients than my female colleagues do. Is it better if survivors are seen by women?

It is not clear from this question whether the counsellor works in a service where the client is given a choice of whether she sees a male or female counsellor. If the woman is given a real choice then she will know what is best for her and this should be respected. My own clinical experience of working in many agencies suggests that women abused by men often select a women counsellor, as do a high proportion of men who have been abused, particularly when this is the first occasion they have come for help. However, it is also clear that when women have a choice, if they choose to see a male counsellor, and if this is a good and boundaried therapeutic relationship, then this is a powerful and helpful reparative experience. So, at the right time male counsellors can help women survivors to form helpful and non-abusive relationships with a man, and learn that it is possible to trust him.

All this is assuming that women have been abused by a man, but this is not always the case. Particularly in the instance of physical abuse, a recent study has shown that mothers are the perpetrators in 49 per cent of cases (Cawson et al., 2000), and many survivors report a horrible combination of abuse from both men and women. But it remains the case that women prefer to be seen by a woman, seeing this as both a safer scenario and one in which it is easier to share intimate and shaming memories. As Hall and Lloyd note (1989), women can find it difficult to express anger to a man and may find it difficult to discuss sexual matters.

It can be argued that male counsellors and therapists can inadvertently re-victimize an abuse survivor because of their own upbringing within a male culture, and because the client has little knowledge and skill in setting emotional and physical boundaries with men. Also, women who have been abused by men tend to give away their power to them, or perceive that they have none. It is also significant that women who have been abused in childhood are a particular target for male therapists who have sexual relations with women clients. Research suggests that up to 20 per cent of clinicians self-reported that they had sex with their clients (Gabbard, 1989), so safety is a significant issue, and problem that is based in reality.

One issue I have encountered in supervising men working with female survivors is that they can underestimate both the extent of the difficulty for the woman in working with a man, and the nature of this. The counsellor may, for example, explore in early sessions the possible difficulties for the woman in working with him, but if she reassures him he assumes that all is well and that this issue has been dealt with. This fails to recognize the extent to which girls abused by men internalize to a very deep, and often unconscious level, the need to be absolutely compliant, never to contradict and always to try to please. Often in their experience of abuse this was the only way to minimize the abuse, or to protect others being threatened if they did not comply. The gender of the counsellor is part of the process: it cannot be dealt with initially and then disregarded, in the same way as establishing time and place to meet is generally only an initial practicality. It needs to be worked with throughout, and the counsellor needs to be listening carefully for clues that their gender may be problematic or inhibiting.

The counsellor also needs to be very aware of his own experiences and feelings – that is, his countertransference. Survivors are expert at recognizing the moods and feelings of others. They have frequently learned to be an emotional barometer in the abusive environment, as they strive to recognize where danger is lurking, in an attempt to avoid or minimize it. They can do the same with counsellors. Any hint that a therapist is uncomfortable with the material, feeling anxious or is unable to cope, will effectively silence the survivor. So the questioner needs to be clear that his own issues do not block his clients.

Sometimes gender, as well as being a genuine stumbling block, may be used as a therapeutic red herring by the counsellor. He cannot change his gender, but he can work on the blocks and difficulties it may produce in him. It is not only clients who sometimes wish to avoid uncomfortable feelings! However, with abused clients these can be painful to acknowledge, particularly if they involve unacceptable feelings of (for example) sexual arousal.

It has been argued that therapeutic style should ultimately be more important than gender. It has also been argued in psychodynamic terms that transference transcends gender (in that transferentially each gender can also represent the opposite gender). But if survivors are to be listened to, it has to be accepted that actual gender really does matter to many. This does not invalidate these other two viewpoints. It does, however, add another crucial part to the equation that must be equally acknowledged. It is also important to recognize that difficulties and issues relating to gender are not just an issue for male counsellors. Female counsellors may over-identify and play the 'rescuer', or may feel helpless and powerless, just like their women clients. Men can similarly fall into the 'rescuing' trap, especially if they experience guilt about being a man, and then wish to over-compensate. There can be pit-falls for men and women, and both genders must be able to identify and examine their own gender-related issues as these particularly affect the way power issues are handled in sessions.

However, the question of choice remains central: both men and women survivors should be able to work with whom they feel most comfortable.

* * *

4.4 I have a client who has very clear memories of sexual abuse from her father and physical abuse from her mother for a number of years until she was old enough to make her protest heard. Since her protest worked she appears to feel she has overcome the effect of those years and she has had previous counselling where she has worked on that. But are there any signs I should be looking for that might indicate that she has nonetheless been left with difficulties?

As this woman is currently a client I assume that she is experiencing some difficulties in her life, although she does not relate them to her abusive ex-periences. As described, the abuse was severe: to be abused by both parents is horrendous for a child, although there may have been support elsewhere – perhaps from siblings, other relatives or from professionals. It seems that when she was able to speak about it she felt she was taken seriously, and hopefully the response she had at the time was a therapeutic and caring one. She also has clear memories of the abuse, so presumably she is not struggling in the murky world of trying to sort out what was real and what was not.

So she remembers, and others believed her and responded. This will not simply have taken away the pain of her experiences, but it will have validated

them. It means she has a full picture of her life and experiences. Her previous counselling, if it was a good experience, provided her with the
opportunity to deal with many of her childhood experiences. However, with
abuse of this nature it would not be surprising if it raised its head again, however positive these helping experiences were, and it is right to be concerned
not to miss this if this is the case.

This counsellor knows the client's presenting issues and something of her
history. The dilemma seems to be how much to follow the path she is presenting, and how much perhaps to follow a sense that surely the abuse is
significant. It may be that the client is right, and currently it is other aspects
of her self and her world that are troubling her. It could be crucial to her to
be seen as a whole person who has many other significant aspects to her
being, other than just being seen as a survivor. It is obviously crucial to the
process that the therapist hears her concerns and responds to them as well
and as fully as possible.

Perhaps a further dilemma is that in knowing her history the therapist is
concerned to be sensitive towards it, not wanting to fall into the trap of being
someone who denies abuse, minimizes it, or would prefer not to know about
it. At the same time, the therapist rightly does not want to invade her inappropriately or push her in a direction that is irrelevant for her. There may be
a dilemma too for the client. Some survivors, especially those who have had
previous and effective help, can desperately want to believe that the abuse
has been dealt with and is now firmly behind them. So they may experience
other difficulties, yet need to believe that these exist somehow in their own
right, unrelated to the abuse and distinct from it. Whilst this can be true, it
may also not be so clear cut. But to the survivor who has felt they have dealt
with it all, it can be a bitter blow if they then recognize that all is not resolved
as they thought and hoped. They may feel right back at the beginning.

So it might be important to explore this and to gently acknowledge that if
therapy discovers that some issues do relate back to the abuse, this does not
mean that progress has not been made, or that the previous help has not
worked. Many difficulties in many people's lives tend to be revisited or are
partially triggered by problems of a different nature. Revisiting earlier difficulties does not mean that the client has to become completely immersed in
them, although this may be their fear. This time, having identified and
worked on difficulties previously can make it easier to recognize and explore
them again. They are like a boulder that has tripped them up, but this is very
different from being a new mountain to climb. However, it may not seem this
way to a client, who may feel that she has failed, or that her previous counsellor has failed, if issues thought to be resolved are still in the way.

In this instance, rather than watching for specific signs that there may still
be difficulties related to the abuse, what may be most helpful is for counsellor and client to look at this as just a possibility, and to consider how the

client would feel if this proved to be the case. The reality that for all of us things that we thought completely resolved are never complete in an absolute sense can be both acknowledged and normalized: things that have been very important may need more attention in different ways at different points in our lives. This is not a failure – each time provides the possibility of moving on, and anchoring the difficulty more securely.

At the same time it is of course crucial to recognize that this may not be the client's experience. The issue she brings could be unrelated, and it is important to respect this. Similarly it needs to be recognized that clients may present with difficulties that are related to earlier traumas, although it may not be helpful or even necessary to go through the initial trauma in too much detail.

* * *

4.5 I work counselling young people aged 16-25. Many are survivors of abuse. Are there particular aspects to this work I need to be aware of?

In working with young people who have been abused it is necessary first to understand the impact of abuse on the young. The age under discussion is a transitional period in development and this has enormous implications for, and impact on, the work. In many ways it is an apt point for therapeutic input: changes and growth can be rapid at this point, although they can also be frightening and anxiety provoking. As childhood, in some senses, is left behind, it is often the first opportunity to seek help independently, and the first opportunity to tell their story. Therefore, an effective response is essential.

Abused children and adolescents have not had the chance to develop normal peer relationships; they have often been precluded from ordinary, everyday experiences. Their boundaries have been invaded, often by the very people they were told they could trust. Their sense of self and self-esteem is often highly negative. The losses to any young person who has been abused are enormous. They have been deprived of many of the normal experiences that contribute to the development of the self and have had few opportunities to form trusting and secure relationships with adults. They have lived in an atmosphere of fear and distrust; their capacity for play and safe exploration of the world and relationships is denied them. It is not easy even in better circumstances to be a young person in today's world, so the normal crises, difficulties and doubts of adolescents are distorted and intensified by abuse. Feelings of alienation and the question of where they fit are particularly painful, as are questions regarding future plans and identity.

In many ways, young people who have been abused and seek counselling at this time are beginning the struggle to accommodate the loss of, and grieving for, their childhood. This is a complex process, particularly if the abuse took place within the family. The young person may in many ways – practically, financially and emotionally – be still wholly or partially dependent on the very people who have hurt them. In other ways too, separating from the family can be highly problematic: essentially safe dependency, the foundation of safe independence, has not been achieved. Home cannot be used as a safe launching pad into the world, and yet there is often nowhere else to run to. Trust has been attacked. A sense of autonomy and of a valued and valid sense of self are often non-existent, and there is little experience of taking risks safely, or that strong feelings can be dealt with non-destructively. Young survivors can feel particularly strongly that they are insignificant and invalid, and that others will use them to fulfil their needs. Their own needs become either peripheral or are not acknowledged at all.

This is normally a time in life when boundaries are tried and tested, and experimentation of various kinds is evident. Young people are in the troublesome business of discovering and setting their own limits, yet this is even more problematic for the abuse survivor who has experienced attack on all of their boundaries, physical, sexual and psychological. They do not have established boundaries, sufficient self-esteem and appropriate trust in others to navigate through this uncharted territory. Contact with their peer group has often been very limited for young victims, and many will have experienced bullying. Abusing and abusive families are often socially isolated, so other models of family life have not been easily visible. Therefore, having a sense of a different non-abusive world may not be available.

This is also a time when exploring sexuality and establishing peer relationships are often a focal point of life, and abuse survivors can find this frightening and alienating. There can be an enormous desire to leave childhood behind: the adult world is perceived as an attractive escape route. It can be hard for counsellors as they recognize how ill equipped young abuse survivors are to join the very world that they think offers them the hope of escape. At this stage of life, negative and positive feelings can be strong and potentially overwhelming – mood swings, unpredictability and conflict are a normal part of adolescent experience, and strain even solid relationships. For survivors who may have nothing solid, life can be very difficult. Questions about future education, employment and where to live add external difficulties to the internal conflicts.

Given this is a vulnerable time in life, the counsellor who works with young abuse survivors can feel a huge responsibility, so what may help facilitate effective and containing work? Some aspects are simply aspects of good practice that should be in place whatever the age group: nevertheless, they have a special significance for this group. Clear boundaries and an awareness of boundary issues is central, recognizing how these have been attacked and how the client is at a point where these are a key developmental issue. The client must feel safe, so clarity on what is offered and assurance of confidentiality are crucial. It must also be properly explained, so the client knows at the outset what is confidential and what cannot be. Reliability is another necessity, even if the client is not: young people do not always appreciate the rules of counselling, and can be casual about timing. Simply providing a different adult role model is in itself therapeutic; being someone who will not abuse, pass judgement, abandon, ignore or deny; and so demonstrates that relationships can be different, and that someone will listen attentively, believe them and take seriously what they say.

A service that is accessible, young person friendly and well publicized in appropriate places is obviously important. It is not easy for young people to wait, so services that do not have waiting lists are most appropriate to their needs. In addition to having an understanding of adolescence, and of the effects of abuse at this age, counsellors also need knowledge and awareness of reality issues such as housing, employment and finance, and how these concerns impact on the young person and on the counselling. The outer world may impinge particularly powerfully. This can pose dilemmas for the counsellor since knowledge of these matters is not usually so vital when working with older clients. There should be good back-up available from other agencies and effective links established with them.

There need to be sufficient trained and supervised staff, as it is important that this is a positive experience for the young person. Skilled assessment needs to be available by well-trained counsellors who are not rigid in their approach. Counsellors need to be able to offer appropriate challenge, for example to destructive behaviours, with the aim of reinforcing the client's ability to make choices and exercise control through increasing insight. Counsellors working in this field with this presentation are more likely to know the identity of abusers and their location. They need to be aware that abuse may be continuing and younger siblings may be at continuing risk. This has considerable implications for the agency and its organization. Clear policies need to be in place regarding these issues, and counsellors must ensure they understand them and work within them.

As adolescence is a stage where acting out behaviour is not unusual, understanding it, and knowing how to respond to it is important, combined with the ability to remain calm and relaxed. It can be particularly harrowing, distressing and anxiety-provoking work. Young people's needs can be expressed urgently and dramatically, although they can also retreat into being deeply withdrawn; acute depression may also be present. There needs to be careful consideration given to the question of sufficient safety nets for the young person if they cannot cope between sessions, remembering that this is a volatile age, where a small difficulty can rapidly descend into a crisis.

When young people are still living with the abuser, it is necessary to consider the complexities of leaving the abusive situation and the abuser. If this is the first time the client has told of the abuse they need a clear message, given at the appropriate time, that it was not their fault. Their pain and the agony needs acknowledging and validating; it clearly must not be denied. It is important to work with the distressed and angry inner child; and to work with regression if this occurs. However, there should never be any force or pressure for such feelings to emerge. The counsellor needs a good awareness of the process of working with abuse, and when appropriate this can be explained to the young person, for example if they experience flashbacks or nightmares.

Counsellors working with abused young people are dealing with the effects of enormous traumas, with clients who are developmentally in a phase of turmoil and deep change. It is important to recognize that, while this creates a potentially problematic and deeply demanding therapeutic situation, this time of huge developmental transition can be an opportunity where there is great potential for change, and where therapeutic input can be most effective.

* * *

4.6 Why does abuse make it difficult for some survivors to separate from their abuser?

Although many survivors successfully separate from their abusers this is clearly a problem for some, as it is for some women who are victims of domestic violence in their adult life. This is not the place to explore this latter aspect, but practitioners who have worked in both areas will recognize some parallels.

It is important to recognize first the impact of abuse on the child and their development. Abuse demolishes a secure sense of self; turns the world into a dangerous place and renders threatening those who are apparently close. The abused child is not given a sense of self-worth and of having a right to a place in the world. Abuse attacks the foundations of the person and does not produce a child and young person who can easily become a confident, autonomous and happy adult. Taking a leap into being an independent, separate person is extremely difficult when what is needed for such a step has never been provided.

A young woman survivor in her twenties, who kept returning to her abusive parents, described this as 'trying to suckle from a dead mother': in order to be separate she still needed what her parents would never give her. On one level she could see this, but on another her deep needs outweighed her objective recognition. Recognizing that for many abused children education has been ruined or adversely affected is also central. Abused children are not good at concentrating, because they are in too much emotional and even physical pain. Achieving educationally is one route away from the abusive environment and some abused children hang on to this tenaciously. Others are too damaged to be able to do so, and another escape route closes.

For younger survivors in particular, the psychological and developmental effects of abuse are further intensified by the practical difficulties in leaving the abuser. If the abuser lives in, or is a frequent visitor to, their home, where is the young person to go? Financial support is limited and accommodation extremely difficult to find even for young people who are confident, resourceful and have backing from supportive parents. Those without it are in a terrible trap, caught between staying in the abusive environment and potential homelessness, which in itself makes them extremely vulnerable and a target for pimps and for further abuse. Many adult survivors are re-victimized as adults by being raped, battered or by being drawn into prostitution (Allen, 1980; Russell, 1986; Bagley and Young, 1987; Briere and Runtz, 1998).

The choices for a survivor are very limited, between a world that offers little and staying with an abuser, who as well abusing may also be proclaiming love and care. Although this dilemma is sharply highlighted for the young survivor it does not necessarily go away with age: in fact the position can simply become more entrenched as the years go by. A woman in her forties exemplifies this position, still living at home with her abusive father, and a mother who apparently did not know of the abuse. Her schooling was seriously restricted because of the abuse; her attempt at a live-in care job at age 18 ended disastrously, because she was sexually harassed by the home owner and had no way of coping. She returned home and remained there. Her father had always assured her of his great love for her, and she had a deeply ambivalent relationship with him. Once back in the home she was financially dependent on him. He resisted all her attempts to socialize, and she had few social skills anyway. Consequently the knot tightened. She finally sought help in her forties but by this time she was a carer for both ill and elderly parents and her depression was profound. It seemed that their death would be the only means of her separating physically from them, and even then psychological separation would be deeply complex.

Other survivors are so convinced, having been so effectively brainwashed by their abuser, that they have no sense of self with which to lead a separate existence. It is as if they have been completely taken over and are in the thrall of the abuser. This is particularly likely to occur when the abuse starts young, where it is extreme in nature, and where the abuser is someone the child is highly dependent on. In effect they are never allowed a separate existence, but exist solely as an object to be used for the satisfaction of another. They have no sense that it could be different. They have a deeply internalized feeling not just of worthlessness, but of having no existence and no rights. This is compounded if the abuse takes place within a ring of abuse where the control of the child and the terror induced is almost inconceivable. Another factor is that the child may have been consistently blamed for the abuse, and the result is a horrible cocktail of self-loathing that may make separation inconceivable. Independence is an unknown and unrecognized concept that is not within their emotional map.

This leads to a further consideration because it is not always the case that survivors do not leave their abusers. It is tragically the case, more frequently than is comfortable to acknowledge, that it is abusers who do not leave survivors. This is particularly the case where a ring has been involved. A victim leaving opens up the possibility of the ring being recognized and thereby coming under threat. Individual perpetrators will go to extreme lengths not to have their activities identified or prevented, but this is minimal compared to the power exercised by a ring. These are clever organizations, often peopled by highly intelligent individuals, including those who have some professional connection to children, with clearly specified plans to prevent discovery. These are people who torture children, who profiteer by making videos of child abuse, who advertise their victims on the net, and who go to extraordinary lengths to prevent their victims from speaking out. Threats are made to the child victim and to the adult survivor. They are told: 'You will never escape from us'; 'We will kill you if you tell'; 'There is noone to tell as we are everywhere'; 'Noone will believe you'; 'We will always know where you are and what you are doing'; or 'You're mad, you'll get put back inside' (a powerful threat for those who have been in the psychiatric system, particularly if this was against their will). These are not false or empty threats, since survivors know the horrors these people are capable of. Sometimes there is no escape and the victim perceives no choice but to stay within the abusive circle. Added to this, both individual abusers, and rings of abusers, are exceedingly skilled at limiting the world of their victim, so that moving out into another realm is actually inconceivable.

A further tragedy for those who do not leave is when practitioners fail to understand the powerful and captivating dynamics that are at work. Statements such as 'She must enjoy it, or else she wouldn't stay with the abuser' are an insult to the survivor and a terrible indictment of the inability of some practitioners to understand the terrible trap that abuse can create. Abuse can capture children. They are not free, but imprisoned by the physical and psychological violence they have encountered. This does not magically disappear in adulthood, and it is a tribute to so many abuse survivors that they do manage to enter other worlds and leave their abusers.

* * *

4.7 Does satanic and ritual abuse really exist?

Even defining the terms in this question is problematic, reflecting the controversies that rage in response to this subject. McFayden et al. (1993) have defined ritual abuse as the involvement of children in many forms of abuse – physical, sexual, emotional – within a religious, magical or supernatural context. Sinason (1994) prefers the term 'satanist' to 'satanic', arguing that this distinction does not incorporate a religious statement about the existence of Satan. The Department of Health in the UK chose the term 'organized abuse' although it also alludes to ritualistic elements: 'some organised groups may use bizarre or ritualised behaviours, sometimes associated with particular belief systems' (1991: 38) However, whilst alluding to this as a possibility it avoids the starkness of ritual abuse, thereby sidelining rather than highlighting the problem. Scott uses the term 'ritual abuse' to describe abuse 'which is highly organised, involves a group of perpetrators, combines physical, emotional and sexual abuse and is supported by a religious or occult ideology ... what sets ritual abuse survivors apart from other survivors of trauma is the sheer extent of the torture and abuse they have endured' (1998: 79). This emphasis on the combination of organization, numbers of perpetrators, extent of torture, and ritualistic context encompasses cogently the extent, nature and horror of this type of abuse.

Given that the history of abuse is fraught with denial, disbelief and controversy, it is hardly surprising that powerful debates take place around this particular issue. Essentially, ritual and satanic abuse and the appalling acts that are contained within it beggar belief. It does not surprise me that many people genuinely and passionately deny that such acts happen, or that such behaviour exists. I would prefer not to believe it myself, and I would passionately prefer to believe that humans are not capable of such evil. However, I find myself forced to believe by the weight of evidence of practitioners I respect and whose work I believe in, and by my own, more limited experience. It may be that at some level I have chosen not to see or not to hear, because the number of cases I have come across where satanic or ritual elements have been involved has been small, but nevertheless horribly real. These cases have also been exceedingly disturbing and traumatic to hear about: they force therapists into a world that they have an extreme resistance to entering, and it does not surprise me that for many this resistance is absolute. Casement notes that:

> For those who hear such accounts, the wish not to believe them is often very acute. To believe what one is being told by a victim of satanic abuse would mean facing something for which one has no adequate means to deal with or to explain. It means accepting that there could be human beings capable of behaving in ways so evil that we cannot bear to conceive of such a possibility. It means facing an outrage to all that we have come to regard as human. (1994: 23)

The ritualistic satanic abuse cases I have heard about in my own experience as a therapist have often involved groups of highly respected and apparently respectable people. A crucial aspect of working with any survivor of abuse is trust. Abuse by someone deemed by society to be trustworthy is a feature of the experiences of many abuse survivors; therapists and counsellors are similarly viewed as trustworthy. This creates a dynamic that inevitably questions and challenges the nature of trustworthiness, and this is even more apparent in ritual satanic abuse. It is intensified by the very nature of the abuse, by the extent of its organization and by the identity of those involved.

Working with such presentations are problematic: 'Ritually abused patients have experienced concrete enactments of very violent scenarios of murder, dismemberment and cannibalism, which for other people are merely phantasies. This leads to a blurring of the distinction between phantasy and reality' (Mollon, 1994: 145). The demands on the counsellor are obvious. I know of one worker, experienced in the field of abuse, who gave up this work on hearing of ritual abuse. It was just too much to cope with. It is certainly not work to struggle with alone: a system of support, of knowing others working in the same area, and of extremely good and knowledgeable supervision are all necessary. Dealing with survivors who have undergone such appalling experiences is deeply stressful and shocking (Youngson, 1993). Practitioners can be so appalled, and become so traumatized that, as the survivor often also experiences, they find that words fail them: they too cannot speak, and they are trapped into silence. Just hearing about such cases can be deeply isolating and alienating, and this has to be redressed by support that is quickly available, reliable and robust. Hearing detail such as is encountered in ritual satanic abuse attacks one's sanity and one's reality. It can be a deeply disturbing, terrifying and horrific experience.

The question is often raised whether such truly appalling accounts of such extreme abuse are really true. It is argued that there is rarely actual evidence (although indeed in work with most survivors this is the case), so how can we safely believe these stories of ritual, torture and murder? There is an excruciating and fine balance at work for the practitioner. The careful and responsible therapist avoids being suggestive to the client, whilst simultaneously wanting to validate the client's own terrible reality. The therapist also recognizes the possibility that some images may be metaphorical rather than literal, although such an explanation may be the therapist's welcome escape route into denial and rationalization. This is all taking place within the context of working with a client who also may not want to believe (a fact that is often ignored by those who dispute that this type of abuse takes place) and who is also caught up in the fantasy versus reality debate. This therapeutic dilemma is vividly and sensitively captured by Mollon in his discussion of 'epistemological terror' (1998: 141).

The lobby that denies the existence of satanic and ritual abuse is a powerful one, often linked to the similarly controversial question of whether recovered memories of abuse are true or false, planted by over-zealous and powerful therapists. Those who argue against ritual abuse argue that there have never been any corroborated cases. Noting the lack of corroborated cases, Schacter et al. state that 'the most reasonable interpretation of these facts is that most (and quite possibly all) recovered memories of satanic abuse are illusory' (1997: 77). Others see the ther-apist as central to the development of the idea of ritual abuse: 'the therapists who specialize in satanic-abuse stories first focus on vague feel-ings or intrusive images and slowly build evidence for the satanic narrative' (Offshe and Watters, 1995: 182). This picture is in stark con-trast to the actual accounts given by the practitioners quoted above, as they vividly describe their struggle to respond to their clients, all too aware of the complexity of issues involved and the therapeutic dilemmas inherent to this process.

For practitioners who encounter this issue it is important to be alive both to the nature of the debate and to what experienced practitioners tell us about the impact of this type of work on them. It is crucial to recognize that it may be possible to implant memories by irresponsible and careless practice that is over-suggestive, particularly by practitioners who are unable to contain ambiguity and uncertainty. However, this does not mean that rit-ual and satanic abuse does not exist. Both can be true. It is also crucial to face our own denial and our own desire not to believe it. The failure to rec-ognize these aspects of ourselves and our society has in the past led us to refuse to see and hear painful truths, including child abuse itself, by dis-torting horrific realities into something more comfortable.

* * *

4.8 In my work with abuse survivors I have noticed that the theme of death often presents itself, although in different ways. Suicidal thought is one of these, but there are others. How can this be understood and worked with?

The struggle between the will to survive and the desire to escape into death and oblivion is one frequently expressed by survivors of abuse. The theme of death is painful both for the client and for the counsellor, and as a result can all too often be denied or avoided. Through encountering, facing and meeting with this aspect of another person we can be faced with uncomfortable, despairing, destructive and damaged parts of ourselves. That death is an inevitable part of life is a truism and it is hardly surprising that struggling with the concept of death occupies a central role for many key theorists, as well as throughout the wider culture of literature and the arts. Klein's concept of innate envy (1975) derives from Freud's death instinct (1920): envy aims to destroy what is good. Rosenfeld (1971) describes destructive narcissism, seen as a manifestation of the death instinct, which organizes a mafia-like gang around the life-seeking part of the personality, and attempts to prevent the client relating to the therapist. Erich Fromm (1991) wrote extensively about human evil and developed the concept of necrophilia, a love of death.

However, the theme of death has a very particular and inevitable significance for many abuse survivors, resonating deeply with much of their early experience. Bettelheim (1980) was very clear that while the psychotic individual can have an internal delusion of a malevolent destroyer, the survivor faced such a person in their real outside life; and Shengold (1979) argues similarly in his discussion of 'soul murder'.

The extent to which different theorists accept the reality of trauma and its impact rather than focus on internal experience is a major debate. Much of the early analytic theory emphasized internal infantile conflicts, and generally it is only more recently that actual destructive attacks on the child have been recognized. One exception to this was Ferenczi, writing in 1932, although his paper remained unpublished, unaccepted and widely unacceptable until it was published in 1955. What is undoubtedly true for children who suffer abuse is that they experience directly the destructive impulses of others, which many theorists understand as solely being contained within the sphere of fantasy.

Exploring the child's experience of abuse can clarify the significance and source of the theme of death and destruction and the different forms this takes. It is not only sexual abuse that needs to be considered. For instance, a mother who neglects and does not respond to a small baby desperate for feeding can ultimately cause the baby to die of starvation; and even if fed, this baby may fail to thrive if other conditions of love, care and attention are not also provided. Children can be killed off psychologically even if physical life is maintained. Similarly, when children are left unattended their cries fade and they fall into passivity – as if hope has died for them. Others experience the continuing and systematic dismantling of the self through constant criticism, constant undermining, invalidation or rubbishing of anything they do or achieve. They are abused psychologically and their sense of self as valid and meaningful is devastated. When the body of a sexually abused child is enveloped by a much larger one, and an object or a penis is forced into them, the child experiences the destructive power of another's body and will. Similarly, with physical abuse: the pain, both emotional and physical, can be so great that some adults recall that as children they either wished for death or feared death.

Some children witness death, or fear a parent or sibling may be killed. A child who lived with the ongoing fear that father would kill mother awoke one day to find a policewoman standing over her bed: her father had finally killed her mother. Other children experience threats of death: to themselves, or to someone close, or to their pets – some adults have described being forced to watch pets being killed or tortured. The disassociated experiences of abused children and adult survivors, which one described as 'going on the ceiling and looking down on myself', are similar to the near-death experiences that some people have graphically described.

Death in a literal sense can be present and real: it can be experienced as a possibility or probability, a threat or a desire, and sometimes it is witnessed. Some child victims and adult survivors attempt suicide. Others are particularly accident prone, or have a high rate of illness. But this is only part of the experience of the child who is abused. As noted with reference to neglect and emotional abuse, psychical death is also significant, where the self, or part of the self, experiences annihilation. There are many examples of this.

It is recognized that many abuse survivors have enormous gaps in their childhood memories. Their experiences are too painful to allow into consciousness, so they have had to be obliterated, and with them large parts of their life at the time have been annihilated. For others, parts of themselves are killed off: the ability to form or maintain relationships, or to trust and allow good things to happen. Some survivors feel unable to have children, others have bodies that are too damaged for child bearing, whilst some fear their children will inevitably be doomed.

Not only does the abused child experience such horrors; they also frequently face denial or blame from the perpetrator, and frequently from their wider world. This adds to the sense of destruction of self, invalidation, non-reality, deep confusion, and the inability to trust the self or judge the world.

Such denial leaves the child few psychological choices and suggests an important question: when such destructive reality is not owned by the perpetrator or recognized by others, where does it go? It has to go inside the person: the experience of the violence, badness, destructive and the murderous, are introjected. If it is too much to contain, splits into different selves can result, each holding different fragments of the experience and memories (Walker and Antony Black, 1999): the possibility of the person becoming integrated perishes. Once internalized, these parts can operate in several ways. They can be turned against the self, and the risks of self-harm, suicide attempts and successful suicide are high in abuse survivors. Similarly, other self-destructive behaviour is also common: drug and alcohol abuse, the attraction to violent or unsatisfactory relationships, or the destruction of those relationships that promise the possibility of good or nourishing experiences.

An example of behaviour that is dangerous and involves unnecessary risks is here given by an incest survivor:

> For a couple of months I had been playing chicken on the highway with men and finally I was involved in an accident. I had not really been dealing with any of the incest issues. I knew vaguely there was something there and I knew I had to deal with it and I didn't want to. I just had a lot of anger at men. So I let this man smash into me and it was a humbling scene. I was really out of control when I got out of the car, just raging at this man. (Herman, 1992: 40)

This is a good example of how destructive feelings can be introjected, resulting in the desire to damage or destroy the self; or projected into rage against others, and in this instance coming together in a highly dangerous combination.

For an abuse survivor, suicidal action can represent both an attractive means of escaping the horrors of life, and a much feared option – as though the person has no will to resist suicide. Some describe it as a force beyond themselves that is dragging them towards death. This is a powerful image that recreates the abusive experience of having no control, but of being under the power of another, often accompanied by the threat of death to the survivor or another person close to them. The fear that accompanies this sense of being dragged towards self-destruction is enormous, yet also difficult to convey, perhaps explaining how problematic and painful it is for counsellors, therapists and other professionals to meet with and work with this aspect. There are other routes for these destructive and murderous parts. They can be projected outwards into anti-social action: this may involve hurting or attacking others, or damaging or destroying property. Child abuse is responsible for a wide variety of social ills. Of course, for others there is a different response: becoming a carer; or becoming a very good parent. These appear to be valid and creative responses to abuse, but even such choices can be understood as including a desire for both revenge and reparation.

Survivors of chronic childhood trauma have to grieve enormous losses: not only what they needed and wanted, and which may have been temporarily or partially experienced but then lost; but what was needed and wanted and never known. Grieving in this situation is exceedingly complex. They must mourn the loss of the foundation of basic trust and the belief in a good parent. The process of unravelling the unconscious internalization of experiences of destruction and their consequences, and beginning to place the responsibility externally, is extremely hard and painful. As survivors recognize that they were not responsible, they begin to confront an existential despair. Shengold (1979) sums this up: 'Without the inner picture of caring parents, how can one survive? Every soul-murder victim will be wracked by the question "Is there life without father and mother?"'.

The following example, told by a survivor, illustrates the layers and complexity of the twin themes of death and abuse: Katy's world had been characterized by violence, which had resulted in both a psychical death for her, and actual death within her family. Her father had consistently attacked her mother, Katy and her siblings from an early age. She described her life as a living death. As a young adult Katy was someone who could feel deeply suicidal, and who came to counselling with a history of both overdosing and cutting herself, as well as of illness and accidents. Some of the illnesses arose directly from the injuries inflicted by her father. Some of the accidents came from being 'phased out' – partly caused by some brain damage, and partly from her habit of disassociating. If life became stressful she would 'leave the scene', thereby making herself very vulnerable, particularly if she then drove her car. Another part of her could at times firmly believe she deserved to die, that she was inherently bad, and that therefore her suicidal feelings were appropriate and reaffirming. At other times she was very frightened by them: she felt as if someone else was controlling her and dragging her to her death. She described this as a magnetic force impelling her to her doom. But these feelings could also be a relief – partly that she could feel something and therefore knew she was still alive; and partly because she felt there was a way out. This was particularly so when she felt overwhelmed by memories and flashbacks that were extraordinarily violent in content.

At these desperate times, when Katy experienced the possibility of death as real, it felt essential to work with her to understand these feelings, and help her to place them within the context of her own experience. This was agonizing work. Primarily the counsellor needs the ability to stay near the most despairing part of the person, without becoming infected by their own despair, and without becoming defensively distant or abusive. Helping the client to make sense of the desire for death, or of their fear of the unavoidability of death, requires recognition and acceptance that these are valid parts of the psyche. The counsellor needs to invite the client to move nearer to these parts of the self, to share them, to allow them to speak, to enable them to be heard, and to express the thoughts, beliefs and memories that the survivor thinks can never be safely shown to anyone. Often they have not even been able to face these themselves – no wonder they become translated into such a force for self-destruction.

The abuse survivor may have lived with the reality of the possibility of death, in a way that most of us do not. This may make death a more likely resolution to adult difficulties: it is a familiar idea, one which they have known and cannot be easily unknown. It can be associated with a deep sense of not deserving to exist; or deserving only a life that is extremely conditional and extremely vulnerable.

This existence is easily shattered by any external circumstance that validates the internal experience. One client was deeply attached to a therapist in the context of a therapeutic relationship that many would see as having dangerously broken boundaries. The therapist left unexpectedly at short notice and was unable to allow the expression of the client's very negative, indeed quite murderous, feelings. She became dangerously suicidal. Perhaps if the therapist had been able to allow the feelings to be expressed, and had helped her find that they did not destroy him, however much part of her desired that, the outcome would have been different. But it was not so: once again her experience was denied, and the more positive view of her self that she had tentatively started to build was entirely invalidated by his leaving. She faced abandonment when she believed she had found safe attachment, and she was convinced this must be caused by her badness. The result was the fantasy of killing him, as well as the desire for her own death.

Death may be feared. It may be longed for. Or both feelings may be present. It may be seen as desirable, or as unavoidable or as simply deserved. It may at times be the only perceived way of giving up on the internalized bad self and fantasized good parent: because it is too hard to bear the opposite truth that it is the other who has been bad. The experience of parents or carers who wanted to annihilate the child leaves the adult questioning their right to live, their ability to live, and their wish to live. The desire and the right to life need a sufficient sense of self-worth and self-respect which we would expect from good enough upbringing, yet these are the very things that abuse erodes and eventually destroys. Death therefore also involves existential death: the death of hope, the death of belief in love and of the world as good, and the death of the possibility not only of good and loving parents but of good and loving relationships.

CHAPTER 5

The effects of abuse on the practitioner

5.1 Do therapists who are themselves survivors of abuse have to be particularly careful when working with clients who have been abused?

There are many services for survivors of abuse that are survivor led. For some survivors it is crucial that when they seek help they know it is from someone who has had the same or similar experiences. It is deeply affirming to have a model of someone who has survived and come through to a position where they can offer help to others. Equally, it is a matter of pride for survivors who become counsellors to feel they can help and empower others, that they have an important role in this process. But other survivors who seek help do not have a strong preference for seeing a survivor.

Perhaps the simplest answer to this question is that everyone who works with survivors should always exercise particular care. There are pitfalls for anyone, and what is important is to recognize that these exist for every individual practitioner, whether or not they are survivors. But what particular pitfalls may exist for counsellors who are also survivors? Perhaps there is a greater possibility of becoming unhelpfully over-involved, with the accompanying danger of the counsellor's own feelings related to their own abuse becoming painfully triggered by the disclosures of the client. If aspects of the counsellor's abuse remain unresolved she may be unable to assist the client with those areas and may become very distressed herself. Another potential problem for anyone seeing any client whose experience resonates very closely with their own is assuming an understanding that may not actually exist. Survivors have survived their own unique experience, and their response to it may be quite different from that of the counsellor who has also survived abuse. So the survivor therapist has to be careful not to assume that she knows when she may not. In exactly the same way, a counsellor who has been bereaved cannot assume that her experience gives her extra or special insight into a bereaved client. Her own experience may indeed block the accurate recognition of issues for the client.

Seeing a survivor therapist can immediately reduce the isolation and secrecy of abuse; it offers hope and possibilities for the future, and can make disclosure easier. Survivors often fear they will not be believed, which in itself can prevent them seeking help. Seeing another survivor removes this fear. What is crucial for survivor therapists is that their own training and therapy has provided sufficient opportunities for exploration of any potential or actual areas of difficulty, and that they have sufficient support in place if difficult issues arise for them.

As shown in response to Question 5.2 working with survivors can trigger strong and problematic feelings for anyone. It may be that within this range of potential difficulties some are more likely to be experienced by survivor therapists, while others are more likely to be felt by their non-survivor colleagues. For instance, counsellors in the latter group often describe a strong sense of guilt that they have been spared such terrible experiences, which may be accompanied by an anxiety about having an easier and enjoyable life. I have not encountered this in survivor therapists. Similarly, I have more frequently encountered amongst survivor therapists a difficulty when memories of their own abuse, previously not available to conscious memory, have been triggered by their work. Although difficult feelings can be triggered in the non-survivor group, they are generally not of the same intensity.

But this question leads to another: is it best for a survivor of abuse if their counsellor or therapist shares their own experience? J. Antony Black, herself a survivor of abuse and who also has multiple personalities, thinks this is not necessarily so:

> I do not believe that counsellors have to have experienced abuse, or to be multiple personality, to work in this area. When I first entered therapy I felt that the therapist could not possibly understand. But ten years on this view has changed. What is crucial is the ability to live in someone else's world without mistaking it for your own. (2000: 123)

She continues to discuss the appropriateness of counsellor survivors with multiple personality working with similar clients. She argues that this is possible only when these counsellors have worked sufficiently through there own issues, otherwise:

> she may become another person who is abusive to the client. The counsellor might then defend herself by avoiding or denying; or she might become traumatised. Splitting on the counsellor's part might result, although this possibility exists in all therapeutic situations where the therapist's unresolved issues are triggered by a client. (2000: 123)

Perhaps what is most important is that the choice exists for survivors: it is clearly an enormous help for some to be seen by a survivor, while for others it is not so important. What is also crucial is for all therapists to be aware of their own areas of difficulty, particularly where these may be potentially damaging to their clients.

* * *

5.2 Listening to some of the narratives of abuse which my clients share with me, I feel sickened and very angry, and sometimes just upset, but know that I mustn't show what I am feeling to the client. How can I best use these feelings to help my clients, but also ensure that they don't make me ineffective by making me feel overwhelmed myself?

As described in Question 5.1, working with survivors is a powerful and potentially distressing experience. To feel sickened, angry and upset, as this questioner describes, is a real, normal, appropriate and human response to hearing stories of terror and torture. However, these responses are also countertransferential, and can valuably inform us about the experience of the survivor. So there are several possibilities in understanding the experience of this questioner. Whilst she describes her own real and understandable feelings as she hears terrible stories, she may also be empathically reflecting what the client consciously feels. She could also be absorbing what the client cannot yet allow herself to feel, which is then unconsciously being projected on to and into the counsellor. A further variation, although not evident in this question, is when the counsellor feels little or nothing, mirroring either the client's desire to minimize the abuse and distance it – a desperate attempt to prevent it from interfering further with life; or dissociation (see Question 3.3) where memories are present but feelings have become disengaged. This latter possibility can also lead to the counsellor feeling overwhelmed, as she absorbs and experiences the feelings that cannot be allowed by the survivor.

So the question is not a simple one. An important first step is to recognize the complexities and possibilities briefly outlined above, in order to assist in monitoring and understanding the processes that may be at work. This is an ongoing issue in the work and not a one-off consideration: trying to identify the source of such powerful emotions is not straightforward, especially where they can spring from more than one source. Recognizing these possibilities goes some way towards preventing the counsellor being overwhelmed or ineffective. Knowing that strong feelings are so informative provides the counsellor with a framework that is purposeful and containing. Another very obvious aspect in ensuring the counsellor is not overwhelmed is the provision of sufficient support with enough time and space to consider their work. So good supervision (see Question 6.5) is vital.

However, the question of how to use these feelings productively and not destructively extends beyond these points. It is crucial that the counsellor is comfortable enough with difficult feelings to allow herself to be open to her experience: denial is dangerous. There is a delicate balance here: on the one hand the counsellor needs to be able to remain in her own experience, to know it, to feel safe with it, and not to deny it; on the other, she must not let her own experience intrude inappropriately on the therapeutic space given to the client. Whilst the therapist monitors herself she also has to prioritize facilitation of the overall process, thus enabling the client to explore freely within a safe and contained therapeutic environment. Scharff and Scharff, writing from an object relations perspective, note that:

> We offer a therapy that is quite different from the patient's experience of suffering the imposition of another person's reality. Instead we leave the patient plenty of room to know and not know, to work and play, to re-experience trauma and to go on being. We work together to create a psychological space for self-discovery in the context of a generative relationship. (1994: 67)

So the counsellor uses her experience and feelings to inform her, but does not spill these on to the client in an undigested and unconsidered manner. To do that would replicate the behaviour of the perpetrator who did not own, contain and monitor their feelings and impulses. It is not therefore helpful for the counsellor to simply tell the client how they were feeling. Comments such as 'What you are saying to me makes me very angry and upset' may have a therapeutic role at some point, but enormous care has to be taken to ensure that statements such as these are actually therapeutically helpful, are not invasive or inappropriate and do not simply meet the needs of the counsellor rather than the client. For instance, if anger is highly dangerous to the survivor this type of comment could be quite overwhelming. Some might argue that it models for the client the acceptability of expressing anger, but I remain sceptical. Clients need to reach such points in their own time when they feel safe enough to own and express their own anger. There is a world of difference between a counsellor who carefully and empathically tracks the client and provides an environment in which it is safe to express feelings that are frightening, and one who becomes overwhelmed thereby throwing her own feelings into the therapeutic space rather than considering and understanding their relevance. An intervention arising from an awareness of unexpressed anger can be framed to acknowledge that anger *may* be around, and can be explored when the time feels right.

Other emotions than those in this question are experienced by counsellors working with survivors, and they can all create therapeutic difficulties if unrecognized. The greatest therapeutic danger comes from acting out by the counsellor who, like the child victim, feels unable to understand and control what is happening. It is well documented that clients who have been abused in childhood are at risk of further abuse and re-victimization (see Question 5.5) and great care has to be taken so that countertransference, especially that which is experienced as negative, is not used destructively. Negative feelings are sometimes hard for counsellors to own; they can create feelings of guilt, discomfort and resentment. Anger is often triggered by working with survivors, and if unprocessed might be directed on to the clients, for example for being difficult or demanding. Resentment can be felt towards them for 'making me feel like this', reflecting countertransferentially how the abuser blamed the victim. If acted upon, the counsellor can become abusive. Another potential problem with countertransference can result in the counsellor ending the counselling prematurely. The counsellor becomes increasingly exhausted, feels helpless and impotent, seems to have tried everything, and nothing has apparently worked. This reflects the experience of the abused child who, unable to do anything about the abuse, splits themselves off from the experience.

Another scenario is when the counsellor finds herself unable to speak and cannot tell her supervisor or colleagues what is happening: she feels frozen or paralysed, and unable to take up or use support. This reflects yet another experience of the abused child or the adult survivor, who cannot speak of or describe what has occurred. A further example is when the counsellor is physically present with their client but emotionally withdrawn. They offer technically correct but therapeutically unhelpful interventions. This mirrors the position of the non-abusive parent, who appears to function appropriately as a parent but actually fails to see or address the real distress. Counsellors can also dread sessions, just as the client had dreaded the abuse. The counsellor in effect becomes persecuted by the client, as the client was persecuted by the abuser. There is then a danger of the counsellor either becoming helpless like the child, or eventually retaliating by also becoming persecutory like the abuser.

Sexualized and eroticized countertransference feelings are not uncommon and are often accompanied by fantasies of rescuing or saving. If unacknowledged, understood and contained, boundaries can wobble and may completely collapse into a sexual relationship. This can be falsely justified by framing it as 'a good loving experience', 're-parenting', or 'a positive, caring, loving relationship with the only person who knows her well', just as the original perpetrator justified his or her actions. Boundaries can similarly collapse by attempting to become the all-loving, all-giving, idealized parent whom abuse survivors long for and need. More time is offered; phone calls between sessions are made; or contact over holidays occurs, not as thought out therapeutic responses or plans but as reactions to an unrecognized countertransference. Boundaries disappear and the safety of the therapeutic space is compromised or destroyed.

A myriad of feelings and countertransferences are encountered in work with survivors and the answer to this question gives an indication of some that are frequently experienced. In themselves they are not unhelpful: they can provide powerful insights into the experience of both the child victim and the adult survivor; if used correctly they can greatly assist the work by spotlighting areas to be worked on. They may also demonstrate to the counsellor areas of their own psyche of which they need to be aware. Countertransference can be either a helpful tool or a destructive weapon. As stressed earlier, feeling strongly about abuse is perfectly valid. It is making sense of feelings that is the key, not eradicating or ignoring them.

* * *

5.3 Sometimes I can't get some of the awful things I hear out of my head – they go round and round all evening, and make it difficult to sleep. Should I stop doing this work? Or is it that working with trauma inevitably does this to counsellors?

Working with trauma has the potential to make an enormous impact on workers. Trauma is contagious, so that counsellors and therapists can experience something of the same terror, rage, despair as the survivor, and can be haunted by the memories and the images evoked by the abuse. One counsellor describing how 'it keeps popping into my head and I sort of see what she told me about'. McCann and Pearlman (1990) suggest that working with traumatized clients creates in the counsellor a repetition of the inner world of the survivor. Counsellors may experience symptoms of post-traumatic stress disorder and past traumas may be revived. This has been described by some as 'secondary traumatic stress' (Hopkins, 1992; Kleber et al., 1995) and is described as 'the stress resulting from hearing about the event and/or from helping or attempting to help a traumatised or suffering person' (Kleber et al., 1995: 78).

Counsellors can thereby experience the replaying of the client's abuse in dreams or flashbacks, and their personal relationships can be disrupted.

Other frequent responses are anger that can become too extreme and too uncontrollable, and a real and profound grief that can feel overwhelming. 'Witness guilt' is another aspect – guilt in the counsellor that he or she was spared these dreadful experiences, a feeling that makes enjoying life difficult, and can potentially lead to counsellors ignoring, minimizing or denying their own needs. This guilt can be intensified for the counsellor, who feels they are causing their client pain by 'making' them go through it all again in counselling. Workers in this field also frequently report dissociative experiences, feelings of depersonalization, bizarre thoughts, and the ending feeling a victim of the client, just as the client feels a victim of the perpetrator. Similarly, counsellors, like survivors, can experience the need to keep it all secret: one therapist commented, 'I can hear things that are so awful I don't want to tell anyone – I don't want anyone else to have to suffer it'.

Both the internal world and the external world of the counsellor can suffer, extending into relationships with others. One counsellor described how she took her little girl swimming and felt unsafe in the swimming pool. She had been hearing from one survivor how her perpetrator had targeted children in playgrounds and swimming pools. Consequently she watched her child closely and constantly, knowing that this was bad for her and that her anxiety was being communicated, adversely affecting her own child's development. Another described how she experienced extreme panic when her teenage daughter was ten minutes late returning one night. Her anxiety was intensified when her daughter commented, not unkindly, that perhaps her mother was doing too much of this work if she was beginning to see danger everywhere, echoing the feelings expressed in this question. Relationships with a partner can also suffer: a woman counsellor who was daily hearing stories of male abuse to women found that on occasions she did not want to speak to her husband, such was her level of rage and disgust; and then she felt guilty. Her husband was deeply supportive of her work, although not all partners are, particularly if they find their ability to support stretched by the strain of living with someone experiencing stress and distress. Another therapist described how her partner would in exasperation ask her why she continued with the work if it upset her so much. This left her feeling isolated and alienated, and that he just did not want to know, like so many people in the lives of her clients.

There can be a sense too of living in a different world from others, one that once discovered and seen can never be set aside. 'Sometimes other people really annoy me, they go on and on about such trivial things and I can feel on a different planet,' is how one counsellor expressed it. She went on to say, 'In a funny way I don't trust the world anymore – I knew before what awful things were done but it's different now I've come face to face with them.' Working with abuse and trauma can indeed be a deeply disillusioning and disturbing process, although it is clear to me, having trained and supervised large numbers of people working in this field, that responses do vary. Some cope with resilience and less distress than others, and remain positive and hopeful, able to contain the work without it contaminating them or their world. Sometimes they feel that their very ability to do this renders them subject to the hostility and disapproval of others.

There is another danger in this work, the belief developing that you must suffer too, and that if you do not you must be defensive, in denial, not caring sufficiently, or not giving enough of yourself. In my experience those who are containing, who recognize and hold the distinction between self and others, who believe they have a right to their own world and enjoyment within it, who recognize and work with exceptionally difficult projections rather than becoming embedded within them, are the ones who can hold therapeutic boundaries most safely and effectively and are able to undertake difficult work without being destroyed.

Working with abuse can be draining and exhausting for the most experienced and resilient counsellor. I write elsewhere:

> Helpers have to be self-protective, whilst remaining accessible and empathic. They have to try and find a position that represents the ideal interface between objective distance and personal involvement, if they are on the one hand to convince the client that they will be with them and will fight for them; and on the other are not to collapse with them. (Walker, 1992: 197)

This is clearly not an easy balance to achieve. It invites the question of what is needed to prevent burnout or undue stress and what is it that enables helpers to manage this work. Part of the answer is to understand the dynamics created by working with abuse survivors, and the deeply unconscious and powerful processes that are at work (see Question 5.2 on countertransference). Understanding the impact of trauma and its character assists in conceptualizing what is happening. It normalizes the responses and feelings evoked by rendering them comprehensible, thereby making them more bearable. The role of supervision is another key, since it can provide a safe space in which to think, to feel and just to be. Space for thinking can be eroded by working with abuse. In a direct repetition and reflection of the experience of the abused child who is overwhelmed and taken over by abuse with no possibility of making sense of what is happening, so the counsellor can become similarly unable to process what is occurring. However skilled the practitioner, this dynamic is potentially always present. As Agass suggests: 'Attributes and skills are unlikely to be effective without the availability of a good enough experience of supervision as a space for containment and psychic processing' (Agass, 2000: 222). Supervision may be one-to-one or in a group – the latter has the distinct advantage of moving away from the dynamic involved in secrets that is central to abuse. The sharing in group supervision can also alleviate the isolation so commonly experienced, as well as providing a valuable forum for sharing ideas, feelings, experience and strategies.

Controlling workloads is also vital – working with trauma is exceptionally demanding and is best done in conjunction with undertaking other work. In agencies where this is not possible, managers of services should take great care and responsibility for ensuring that staff do not carry too many of the most distressing cases. Organizations where a major focus is on working with survivors need to be exceedingly responsible for facilitating and enabling the work of the counsellors. Sadly this is not always the case, and the dynamics of an organization can be counter-productive to counsellor well-being, which ultimately affects the clients (Walker, 1996).

It is also important for counsellors to work within their level of competence. This can be a problem because it is not always possible at the start of any piece of work to gauge the complications that may arise. However, recognizing levels of competence

> is not an easy or straightforward equation but it is in part the recognition *in itself* that this is complex that helps counsellors work within their limitations. Over confidence is dangerous as is a desire to learn too much too quickly with an 'interesting' or 'challenging' client as the unfortunate guinea pig. (Walker, 2001: 122)

The desire to work with a client who is perceived as challenging can be particularly powerful where childhood trauma is part of the picture: as discussed in Question 5.2, the countertransferential desire to rescue can be powerful, and can have damaging effects on the client if thoughtlessly acted upon. It is also very important for counsellors to have a life apart from their work, with space to enjoy themselves and maintain their physical and psychological well-being. Personal support, whether in the form of friendships, therapy, supervision, hobbies and interests, or a combination of these, is essential. Time for self is not an optional extra or a luxury; to care effectively for others, self-care is absolutely a basic need.

All this has to be seen in the context of the trauma of abuse occurring usually in the context of an apparently trusted environment (the home, a school, a children's home, a church, a hospital); of the trauma often being repeated and sustained; of it often involving more than one person; when a child is small and powerless, frequently unable to tell and often directly blamed and threatened. Not surprisingly, therefore, there is a huge psychic and somatic response – a shattering of the self, with the very essence of the self under the deepest threat and the greatest assault. A range of defences come into play which are deeper and more complex in relation to the ongoing nature of the trauma, how often it was repeated, how severe it was, the age of its onset, and the closeness of the relationship that is spoilt.

Traumatic experiences shatter the illusions of safety and security that we need, and their power is such that they are communicated, repeated and projected into other relationships. So if the counsellor in question is experiencing these powerful communications and projections, it certainly does not mean she should stop doing this work, but understandably she and we do need help and support to disentangle the dynamics and free us from the worst excesses of such distressing experiences.

* * *

5.4 I have sometimes wondered whether I could actually work with a client who reveals that he or she is or was an abuser. What emotional and technical factors will I have to be prepared for?

As noted in Question 3.2, there is some correlation between childhood abuse and becoming a perpetrator in later life. This inevitably means that some work with survivors may also involve encountering those who abuse, a possibility that is not always recognized until encountered by the counsellor. Many counsellors describe themselves as working with victims, and not working with perpetrators. Unfortunately in some situations this is not a clear divide and the same client falls into both categories.

A central ethical concern revolves around child protection. Work with a perpetrator may not be able to proceed at the client's pace, as would normally be the case. If there is a real current concern about risk to children this needs to be immediately taken to supervision, where the response might need to be rapid and not in line with the client's wishes:

> We are faced with a dilemma in abuser counselling however, that of relating to multiple clients. Not only must we consider the abuser and his concerns as a focus for our professional activity but we also have to consider society as client also. This is especially so in the case of potential primary and secondary victims of the abuser should he relapse. Our overriding concern must be that of public protection. This means that the needs of individual abuser clients, on occasions, will be outweighed by the needs of others. (Briggs, 1998: 110)

Counsellors in agencies generally work in a context where this ethical issue has been considered, policies formulated and procedures specified. The extent to which clients know of these policies at the start of counselling varies somewhat: in my experience most agencies in their information to potential clients address confidentiality. However, this varies in its details. There may simply be a general statement that there are some circumstances in which confidentiality would be broken, whereas other agencies make specific reference to child abuse as an area that cannot be kept confidential. In the latter situation, if a client reveals that they have abused, or are currently abusing, this may reflect their own recognition that they want and need help; alternatively it may be a challenge to the counsellor and their professional boundaries. Counsellors in agencies therefore have a structure to work within, one that contains them by specifying the limits of their role regarding confidentiality. Those who work in private practice, although beholden to the same legal and ethical systems, are in a position of having to make their own decisions, without having such a clear structure. Either context can cause great anxiety and distress to the counsellor, who is put in a position where the usual central tenets of counselling of confidentiality and that the client controls what, how and when they reveal personal details, may have to be challenged.

Counselling survivors of abuse, as the answers to many of the questions in this chapter suggest, is an emotionally complex task. Paradoxically it also has an inherent simplicity: as long as the inner hurt child remains in sight and the counsellor recognizes that she lies within the adult survivor there is little conflict over where sympathies lie. Child abuse is wrong; it is not the fault of the child or their responsibility. The responsibility lies absolutely with the adult perpetrator. Nevertheless, in this instance where the client is victim, survivor and perpetrator such simplicity does not hold. In its place there is a multitude of conflicting, anxiety-provoking and uncomfortable feelings. This is particularly apparent when the perpetration is revealed later in work where the client has already been defined as a victim or survivor. The counsellor has established rapport in the relationship; the client is a real person who has suffered greatly and cannot easily be dismissed as a faceless and distant perpetrator, someone who can be labelled bad or evil. The counsellor probably already has warm feelings towards the client. It is a huge shock to discover that this same person, whom they thought they knew, behaves or has behaved in ways that are profoundly distasteful. Countertransferentially this is quite a roller coaster.

Working with perpetrators of abuse is essentially different from working with survivors. It is not possible to focus solely on the client: the well-being of others who are vulnerable has to be kept in view. Additionally, there are other aspects to the work not usually present in work with survivors. For instance:

> The client should be made aware of the potential for disclosure of abuse to influence sexual fantasising subsequent to sessions. The client should be discouraged from such sexual fantasising, not least as in simple conditioning – the more the fantasy becomes linked with sexual arousal and ejaculation, the greater the strength the abusive interest will assume. (Briggs, 1998: 113)

Many counsellors have not been trained in working with perpetrators, and yet it is sometimes unavoidable, even when they have actually decided not to work with such clients. It is not always apparent at initial assessment, and may be revealed only when trust has been established. Counsellors may feel at this stage that they both wish to continue the work and have a responsibility to do so. They still need to seek help in this eventuality from those who have experience and expertise in this work. Technical considerations regarding the most effective form of therapeutic intervention come best from those with specific knowledge.

If we take child abuse seriously and want to work with its victims it is obviously vital that effective therapeutic help is also given to perpetrators. This may be the more distasteful end of the work, but it helps to remember that an abuser who has been victimized has also been hurt and damaged, and has not yet resolved their own abuse. In this sense they remain a victim, if not a survivor, and although all necessary measures must be taken to protect innocent and vulnerable children, in order to tackle this appalling problem it is also important not to just turn our backs on perpetrators. It certainly produces conflicting emotions and ethical dilemmas, but it is a problem that will not go away, and needs the input of skilled therapeutic help.

* * *

5.5 I have begun seeing a woman client who was seduced into having sex by her previous male therapist. I like to think that she will be able to trust another woman like me, but I am aware that my gender may not be the main issue. How do I best approach these early sessions?

In a particular two-year period, I encountered two people abused by the same therapist, was told by another that she had been sexually involved with her therapist in an NHS psychotherapy unit, was informed by a suicidal client of her experience as an in-patient on a psychiatric unit where her psychiatrist had blatantly broken boundaries and declared his love for her (and was still sending letters to this effect), and had another client who presented in enormous distress as her previous therapist had just broken off their 'affair' begun when they were in therapy. What all these events have in common is that each of the women had been abused in childhood, the therapists were all senior in their professions, including one in a very eminent position, the therapists were all mature in age though not in their behaviour, and the distress caused was extreme. This profile of abusers is reflected in the literature, which suggests that abusive therapists are predominantly male (Rutter, 1990) and have professional credibility (Strean, 1993). Out of the four therapists known to me, three at the time of writing are still in practice and the fourth, although he resigned from his professional association and left the area where he was practising, may be. Presumably my experience is not unique, but if this is the experience of one practitioner it gives some idea of the scale of the problem.

It is indeed recognized that this is a significant problem (Rutter, 1990; Masson, 1992; Russell, 1993; Cassidy, 1999; Moore, 1999). Clients give moving accounts of their experiences, which communicate powerfully the depth of the betrayal experienced and the pain caused. Wolf (1998) and 'Poppy' (in Casemore, 2001) vividly depict from the survivor's perspective the extent of the damage and agony. In the light of this it is not surprising that in my experience women who have been abused by men in therapy opt for a woman therapist thereafter, as the client in this question does. In that sense, gender is significant, and is likely to provide some feeling of safety. However, I think the questioner is correct in believing this not to be the main issue, even if respecting and honouring her preference is essential (see Question 4.3).

The issues likely to be faced in this situation are considerable: as noted in other answers, it is not always easy for an abuse survivor to seek help. Trusting is deeply problematic and the very essence of the counselling relationship – which involves being in an enclosed space, behind a shut door, in a situation where noone else knows exactly what is happening, in a confidential (secret) context – can be extremely frightening. It may in itself replicate something of the abusive environment. Added to this, the problematic and ambivalent relationship an abuse survivor is likely to have in respect of closeness and intimacy, both fearing yet in other ways desiring and needing this, and the inherent difficulties with boundaries, all join to create a complex context.

To then be betrayed by the very person a client turns to for help is an appalling repetition of the original trauma. Webster notes that:

> To understand the havoc that is caused when therapy becomes abuse we are required to consider what happens when trust is broken. Clients, in trusting therapists with their private feelings and thoughts, must believe what therapist say and do. When therapist actions seem to go against clients' inner sense, it is understandable that the first people they will doubt will be themselves. (1998: 22)

The feelings triggered by the original abuse are replicated and the survivor experiences self-blame, anxiety, guilt, a sense of being bad and dirty, impotent rage, fear and hopelessness. Yet another layer is added if the therapist has promised marriage, or to be a partner, or that he will leave his current relationship for her. The sense of invasion, abandonment and betrayal is huge. For the adult survivor who experienced comfort, excitement or sexual pleasure from the abuse in therapy, the confusion is further intensified, as indeed can be the case for the child victim. Yet another painful turn of the screw is if the abusing therapist, like the childhood perpetrator, has used similar brainwashing tactics: 'You were irresistible'; 'It's what you really wanted'; 'It's just what you need'; 'I'm making up for all the love you've never had'; 'You were so seductive'; or 'It was your fault – you were the one who started it'. Of course, these have a particular potency when addressed to an adult who may indeed feel she did have a part to play. Such tactics conveniently ignore the professional responsibility of the therapist to hold the boundaries, to safely contain the client and to work with material or behaviour that may indeed be very difficult or challenging.

In the case in question, seeing a woman counsellor may feel safer, although the client could see her as someone who is as helpless as she is, another woman who cannot prevent or intervene effectively in her pain. This scenario is particularly likely if the client was originally abused by a man in a context whereby significant women in her life could not, or did not, come to her aid. This may both reinforce and reflect the counsellor's experience of feeling that she can do little or nothing, especially if her client does not to wish to take formal action against the perpetrator, and where the counsellor wishes she would. This is particularly hard for the counsellor where she knows the identity of the abuser, especially if she knows he is well regarded and senior in the profession. It is important that the counsellor does not impose her own agenda here, although she must make it clear to the client that she does have the right to formally complain if she herself decides to. However, the client must be able to make her own decision – her power has already been terribly eroded.

As with good practice in counselling any abuse survivor, it is important that the client is heard and believed, and that it is clearly stated and acknowledged in these instances that it is always the responsibility of the therapist to act appropriately, work within boundaries, and never to re-victimize. Being with a client in this position is very demanding: the counsellor has to deal with her own feelings, whilst supporting the client and working with the material. She has to recognize the level of distrust, rage and despair that may be present, and how this is expressed in the present counselling too. She knows she belongs to the same profession as the abuser, but has to avoid both defensiveness or unhelpfully expressed anger. Another major difficulty is that the focus of the work may stay on the adult abusive experience, although the counsellor is aware that the set of difficulties that brought the client to counselling in the first place are lying dormant and unexplored. They remain as real as they were, although for the time being perhaps inaccessible. Abuse by a therapist can overwhelm the therapeutic space, and whilst counsellors need to recognize this, and the extent of the trauma, they also need to hold in mind these other difficulties, remaining alert for the time when the client is ready to address these.

* * *

5.6 When might a survivor not be suitable for counselling?

Although counselling offered at the right time can be a healing and repara-tive experience it is also clear that this is not necessarily so (Walker, 1992). Counselling is not a panacea or a cure-all: it is not the right approach for all survivors all of the time. It is always important to check with any survivor coming to counselling if it is what they want. Some have been actively encouraged by friends or relatives to come and have been unable to say no. Such encouragement may be actively benign or well intentioned, but it can be perceived as being, as indeed it sometimes is, a demand or an order. Given that coming to counselling is a major, difficult step, the survivor needs to be sufficiently clear that this is what she wants. Some ambivalence is perhaps inevitable and needs acknowledging and validating, but too much doubt makes engagement impossible. For the survivor to come just to please others has echoes of having to please the abuser or face even worse consequences.

Counsellors always need to ensure that the help they offer will not make the person worse. Although some approaches, notably cognitive analytic therapy (Ryle, 1997), work with borderline personality, many counsellors would feel they do not have sufficient or appropriate knowledge and skills to work with such clients. There is, however, even here a note of warning: many survivors have been wrongly or inaccurately diagnosed, and have therefore been incorrectly assumed to be unsuitable for counselling. So counsellors need to be skilled in assessing clients, and be able to say no if they do not feel it is appropriate. They should also have a working know-ledge of other resources that may be better equipped to help.

Counsellors who, for instance, work on a weekly basis and have neither the time, capacity nor the training for greater frequency of sessions need to ensure that the client is able to manage between sessions, and that they have enough support to do so. It can be extremely hard for a client if they do not have a job that provides structure, if they live alone, have few or no friends, or if they have an abuser remaining in their world. When they start to explore painful areas that are distressing, this is sometimes unexpected-ly difficult. Survivors who find it hard to contain how they are feeling between sessions may benefit from linking in with a survivors' group that provides more readily available support. Once-weekly counselling by itself may be insufficient for the client, but if other support is available in addition, this may provide the necessary therapeutic package. The combination of individual counselling and support group can work, although boundaries have to be very carefully established and maintained.

So the question is not just if the client is suitable for counselling but whether the counselling offered, and the context it operates in, matches sufficiently what the client needs. One therapist may not be a good match, but another may be; or a particular therapist may be only if the context is right. A counsellor may work well with a client who is actively self-harming, or is a suicide risk, as long as this takes place in an agency where the client is held and contained; but this may not apply in private practice, particularly one based in the therapist's home. It is important for the counsellor to feel safe, so a client who threatens violence or has a past history of violent behaviour to others is likely to be beyond the scope of most counsellors. Given that many survivors turn to alcohol and drugs, there is a question of whether counsellors should see a client who is obviously intoxicated. My own position is that I do not, but others who work specifically in the addictions field might disagree (see Reading and Jacobs, 2003: 58–62).

Clients who are obviously psychotic are not the right people for counselling. There needs to be a basic sense of sharing the same reality, even if this reality is at times hazy and confused for the client. Clients who expect a magical and instant solution are likely to be disappointed, although sometimes on assessment it is possible to get beyond this to a more realistic view of what counselling can offer. There needs to be a sufficient degree of consensus on the meaning and process of counselling. If this is not in place there is a danger of the counsellor taking on a grandiose, rescuing stance and the client becoming more demanding and needy. Other survivors may find the counselling situation too threatening (where therapy itself has been abusive: see Question 5.5) or cannot tolerate being in an enclosed space with another person. In this instance groups (see Question 6.2) may be more appropriate. If survivors have serious external issues that are totally absorbing and distracting them (e.g. housing, finance) the timing may not be right; advice from those working in these areas can be a necessary prerequisite to counselling.

It is always important to work within one's level of expertise and training. A survivor who finds working with words difficult but likes to work in a medium of art, music or drama needs to be referred to someone with that training. There is a world of difference between appropriately incorporating some of these techniques into the work when it is helpful for the client, and working throughout in this modality. Dabbling is dangerous. Techniques can be powerful both negatively and positively, but are more

likely to be damaging in untrained hands, however enthusiastic the counsellor is.

It is of course far from pleasant to say no to a survivor in need. But it has
to be said sometimes, remembering the havoc and pain that can be caused
by irresponsible intervention.

* * *

5.7 I am very concerned at the threat of complaints, or even legal action, when talking about abuse is sometimes construed as planting false memories. What is false memory syndrome? Can memories really be repressed?

Abuse continually poses a challenge to what we think and believe of our fel-
low human and it is inevitably therefore a controversial area. One of these
controversies relates to issues of the repression of memory; of subsequent
recovered memories and whether false memories can be created in their
clients by counsellors and therapists. This causes great concern to survivors of
abuse, to those who work with them and to families who believe themselves
wrongly accused of abuse. There is a potential danger in the debate that it may
also prove to be an escape route for perpetrators. As Herman points out:

> In order to escape accountability for his crimes, the perpetrator does every-
> thing in his powers to promote forgetting. Secrecy and silence are the per-
> petrator's first line of defence. If secrecy fails, the perpetrator attacks the
> credibility of his victim. (1992: 8)

I myself choose not to use the term 'false memory'. This reflects my view
that serious and proper debate is needed on this subject and that all too
often a highly emotive presentation prevents this from happening. The
term 'false memory' is in itself emotive, suggesting that the memories
referred to *are* false. When, as often happens, the term 'syndrome' is also
attached, a pseudo-scientific validity is implied that is neither accurate nor
helpful. The term 'false memory' was originally coined in the USA after a
woman, Jennifer Freyd, recovered memories of childhood sexual abuse
whilst in therapy. Her parents disputed the accuracy of her memories and
in conjunction with Ralph Underwager started the False Memory
Syndrome Foundation (FMSF). They believe that otherwise healthy families are being destroyed by ill-trained therapists who may actively seek to
discover in therapy, particularly by the use of hypnosis and 'truth drugs',
repressed memories of abuse that are essentially false.

Dr Ralph Underwager was well known in the USA before his involvement with this group for acting as a defence witness in over two hundred cases of child sexual abuse. A study carried out by Anna Salter, and supported by the New England Commissioners of Child Welfare Agencies, studied the accuracy of his 'expert testimony' and examined the literature he referred to, which apparently strongly supported his arguments (Salter, 1989). She discovered many inaccuracies, including research that was inaccurately quoted, minor findings quoted out of context that when taken in context would not have supported his position, extrapolation beyond the limitations of the data, and ignoring contrary evidence. Underwager (1993) also published an interview in the Dutch magazine *Paidika – The Journal of Paedophilia* in which he was asked if choosing paedophilia is a responsible choice for the individual. He replied:

> Certainly it is responsible. What I have been struck by as I have come to know more about and understand people who choose paedophilia is that they let themselves be too much defined by other people ... Paedophiles spend a lot of time and energy defending their choice. I don't think a paedophile needs to do that. (Underwager 1993: 3)

Although following the publication of this article he resigned from the FMSF, nevertheless the credibility of any group in which the founder argues in favour of paedophilia must be severely in doubt. The group rapidly gained momentum in the USA, with people taking up strongly adversarial positions on both sides of the argument. The British False Memory Society was set up in 1993 by Roger Scotford, who had been accused by his two daughters of sexually abusing them in childhood. This group is also adamant that unscrupulous and under-trained practitioners are able to plant false recollections in their clients, and that the lives of innocent families are being ruined as a result of the consequent accusations made against them. Much of the attack from the False Memory Society is against therapists, who (they argue) strongly suggest to their clients that they have suffered childhood abuse. Whilst it is important to recognize that false allegations of abuse are possible and do occur, there is also a valid concern that it could be a convenient abusers' charter. It is well known that perpetrators of abuse are highly likely to deny their offences, and even continue in this denial after conviction (Kennedy and Grubin, 1992).

The British Psychological Society report on recovered memory (1995) reviewed the relevant literature; they surveyed their members and scrutinized the records of the British False Memory Society. The report notes that most public attention is concerned with memories recovered in therapy, but in fact most clinicians working in this field are counselling survivors who come with memories of abuse, and that in many cases the abuse has been verified by another person. The BPS survey gives some indications of actual occurrence. Of those questioned, 90 per cent had seen clients in the past year who had reported child sexual abuse. One-third said clients had recovered memories before therapy, and about 20 per cent had seen at least one client who had in the previous year recovered a memory of abuse. What is not clear from this figure is whether or not this 20 per cent actually presented with some existing memories of abuse. An interesting result from this survey is that a third reported clients recovering a memory of a traumatic experience other than abuse. In the BPS analysis of the 97 cases recorded by the British False Memory Society, only half had enough information to allow crude statistics to be extracted. In half of these there was explicit mention of memory recovery from total amnesia, i.e. a quarter of the total. The BPS survey is a sensible document, providing a useful and careful framework with sound and careful guidelines for practitioners.

An important question surrounds the possibility of the repression of memory. Sargant (1967) reported that during World War II there were many cases of what he called acute hysterical losses of memory. Research by Herman and Schatzow (1987) found that 64 per cent of women with self-reported histories of sexual abuse, most of whom had corroboration from other sources, had incomplete or absent memories of their abuse at some time in their past. The more violent the abuse the greater the degree of memory impairment. The authors comment:

> Marked memory deficits were usually associated with abuse that began early in childhood, often in the pre-school years, and ended before adolescence. In addition, a relationship was observed between frankly violent or sadistic abuse and the resort to massive repression as a defense. (1987: 5)

Linda Meyer Williams (1992) studied 129 women with previously documented histories of sexual victimization in childhood. In other words, abuse had been proved to have taken place. In detailed interviews a large proportion of the women did not recall the abuse, which had actually been reported 17 years earlier. Women who were younger at the time of the abuse, as well as those molested by someone they knew, were more likely to have no recall of the abuse. In one case a woman told the interviewer that she was never sexually abused as a child, although her uncle had sexually abused her when she had been 4, as well as her cousin aged 9, and her friend also aged 4. In addition to the research, survivor accounts give further weight to the argument for amnesia in respect of childhood abuse. An example of complete repression of a traumatic and painful childhood is found in *No Longer a Victim* by Cathy-Ann Matthews (1986).

The question arises that if memories can be repressed what is it that allows them to surface? Clinical experience suggests many factors may be at work here: one is that the individual's tolerance level increases as their external world becomes safer and more secure. One not unusual pattern of recall is that it occurs after the abuser has died and cannot therefore be directly accused or prosecuted.

There is a danger, intimated in this question, that the ability to work with disturbing and distressing material will be undermined by the fear in counsellors of having allegations of implanting false memories made against them. The following guidelines might help. First, it should never be assumed that those presenting with issues other than abuse have been abused just because the clinical material may suggest the possibility. An example is clients who present with eating disorders. Although research has shown (Oppenheimer, 1985) that two-thirds of women with bulimia had been sexually abused before the age of 15, abuse cannot be diagnosed or assumed on the basis of an eating disorder. Similarly, lack of recall of childhood events may suggest abuse, but it is not the only explanation.

Second, counsellors are now quite rightly very aware of the numbers of clients presenting as survivors of childhood abuse, and as more is written and researched they have more knowledge of how this might be manifested. But any knowledge must be used with care, with the recognition that knowledge is never absolute. There is a twin risk: one is that counsellors deny the level of abuse and its effects, particularly when abuse is severe and horrifying. The other is that the counsellor, in an anxiety to create certainty in the midst of chaos and confusion, may over-emphasize or wrongly interpret certain aspects of the client's experience, in order to provide a definite explanation that perhaps counsellor and client both want and need.

Third, counsellors need to recognize the strength of language – abuse is a powerful word with very particular connotations currently. It should not be used unless the client does so. The pace of the work should always be set by the client: if they are using phrases such as 'Things weren't easy when I was little', or 'Bad things happened to me', this is also the level at which the counsellor should respond. To reframe these types of comments in terms of the client having had abusive experiences, before the client recognizes them as such, is invasive and inappropriate. The client can be asked, for example, if they want to tell you a little more about things not having been easy; but this should also be accompanied by reassurance that they can take their own time over whatever they want to talk about.

Fourth, although most abused clients come with some memories, and recall more as they begin to deal with the abuse, and some come because they have recently recovered memories, there are those who actually recover memories in counselling. This can be deeply shocking for the client and for the counsellor, and it is important to respond calmly. There are particular memories that act like a log-jam – once they are dealt with and the fear surrounding them is allayed, the client may be free to recall others. In this way a retrieved memory can start a whole process of remembering.

This is neither comfortable nor easy: there can be great resistance, as enormous pain is likely to be encountered, and threats in the past not to tell have often been well internalized. If the client wants to act on these memories by taking legal action or by confronting the perpetrators, counsellors should encourage the client to take their time with these major decisions. Counsellors should not *advise* action: this breaks the boundaries of the work and is beyond their expertise.

Finally, the use of hypnosis to aid the recovery of memories is a fraught and emotive subject. I have worked with a client who recovered memories under hypnosis when the training of the hypnotist had been limited to a correspondence course and two weekend workshops. She had no idea how to work with the material or the regressive state that emerged. In this case the recovered memories were not entirely accurate; some details were distorted, although in essence they were true and were verified by an older family member. At the other end of the scale, some very experienced clinicians regard hypnosis as a means of re-integrating dissociated parts of the self. There is a huge difference between experienced and highly trained clinicians employing this as one tool amongst many, and those who are inexperienced playing with a powerful technique. The rule of thumb should be that unless highly trained both as a hypnotherapist *and* in the field of abuse, do not use hypnosis. My own perspective is that I work with recovered memories if they emerge, and I work with regression similarly; but I do not use techniques actively aimed at precipitating these. It is worth repeating that the client must set the pace.

My own clinical experience in this field suggests that the proportion of clients who recover memories, having started from a base of no memories, is small. However, gaps in memory of varying degrees of severity are commonly reported amongst those who have suffered abuse in childhood, and those who have experienced other forms of trauma.

There is clearly a real concern at the possibility that false memories can be induced in the therapeutic setting, particularly when certain techniques are employed; and this concern must be taken seriously. The volatility of some of those who are most actively involved in forwarding the notion of false memory is not helpful, and counsellors need to address the issue without becoming caught up in highly emotional arguments. As in all their client work, counsellors should not be suggestive, nor should they jump to rapid conclusions. Perhaps what is most important is that they should be able to tolerate and work with uncertainty. This controversy need not distract us from working with survivors of childhood abuse, nor undermine it.

* * *

5.8 I am realizing that one of the men referred to by my client as abusing her is still working with children. Should she report her suspicions to the police? Or should I? What do I need to do in terms of the Children Act?

The context the questioner is working in is unclear, although context is very significant in answering the question. It is specified under Section 47 of the Children Act 1989 that those employed in police and social services have a statutory obligation to report and investigate when there is 'reasonable cause to believe that a child living or found in their area is suffering or likely to suffer significant harm'. Although the client is referring to a past incident, the abuser may be a continuing risk to children. If this counsellor is employed by social services it is very clear that this concern should be relayed to the appropriate person for a decision to be made regarding the requirements of the Act and for child protection investigation.

However, the situation is not so clear-cut if the counsellor is working in some other contexts. The statutory obligation to report and investigate child abuse does not extend to counsellors employed in other settings or working privately, although counsellors working in any setting bound by local authority rules (for example, education, health, housing) are expected to liaise with social services, and to assist them by providing relevant information and advice. Both the Children Act and the guidance document 'Working Together Under the Children Act 1989' recommend inter-agency co-operation (Department of Health, 1991). Any counsellor working in such agencies should be very clear from the outset of their employment about the guidelines they are required to work to. These should be discussed both with their line manager and with the counselling supervisor in terms of their implications for confidentiality in regard to child protection. Counsellors should take responsibility for ensuring they have read and understood any guidelines that are available. To some extent, forewarned is forearmed: the situation described in this question is exceedingly anxiety-provoking and counsellors need to be aware of any limits to their work.

As there is in the United Kingdom (unlike the United States) no mandatory reporting of child abuse, the counsellor in this question, if not employed directly by social services or by an agency bound by their regulations, is left with a moral dilemma which in turn leads to a choice of action. The counsellor may be caught between two principles – the desire to ensure and uphold the privacy and confidentiality of her client, and her desire to protect other children. Knowing that abusers reoffend over a long period of time, that the rate of recidivism is high, and that an individual offender may have a large number of victims (Soothill and Gibbens, 1978;

Burgess et al., 1981; Carnes, 1983) indicates that this perpetrator is highly likely to be a danger to children, especially if he is in a job where access to children is easy.

Discussing this dilemma in supervision is the obvious first step; a second is to explore the dilemma with the client. Clients know from their own experience of counselling that their abuse has been taken seriously, and may be very aware that revealing this type of information will also be taken seriously. The client may have decided to disclose for this very reason: she consciously or unconsciously wants action taken to protect other children. Deciding what to do should always be done in consultation with the client unless very exceptional circumstances dictate otherwise. Any action taken should preferably be with their agreement. If the client decides to report her concerns, unless she does so anonymously, this could involve her in an ongoing process, involving intimate and distressing revelations about her own experiences of abuse. It is vital to support her throughout, even though at the beginning of this process it is not possible to predict what course it will take, how long it will continue, what it may involve, or what the outcome will be.

My experience of clients taking action against abusers is extremely varied. One young woman who reported her abuse to the police felt vindicated and empowered when investigations led to her abuser being prosecuted and imprisoned. Another young man similarly went to the police, but they did not have sufficient evidence to proceed. However, he felt understood, taken seriously and respected, and most importantly for him he felt that he had done all in his power to protect other children, even if ultimately this had not proved possible. But another woman had a very different experience of reporting the identity of her abuser to social services. He still lived nearby and she was sure he was involved in an abuse ring. However, three days after giving them the information she was told it had been investigated and there was no cause for concern. She felt betrayed again by the system and did not believe they could have undertaken a proper investigation in that time. Another young man, abused by his step-father (a teacher and a scout leader), felt his younger brother was at risk. He too was devastated when, after contacting the NSPCC, he was assured there was no cause for concern. It is of course difficult to know if these latter assessments were correct, but in the case of the young man he had always felt that the professional status of his stepfather and his charming, educated and convincing manner had always prevented anyone recognizing him as a perpetrator. This inevitably reflected precisely the view of his stepfather: he was convinced he was invincible. In his disappointment the young man left counselling. His stepfather refused to allow him back in the house and the young man wished he had said nothing, since he had been left further demoralized and isolated.

If the client in question does not want to report the abuser she may want the counsellor to do it for her. This does not involve the counsellor with a dilemma of breaking confidentiality as she is then acting with her client's permission. Although she would still need to work with the effect of this in the counselling, as the dynamic of the relationship is undoubtedly changed by these types of interventions, nevertheless the situation would then be relatively straightforward. The client and the counsellor would know that they had done all they could to protect children; that others were responsible for carrying out the investigation; and that the counsellor has taken the client seriously and had not had to break confidentiality.

A real difficulty arises, however, if the client does not give permission. The counsellor has to ask herself if she will be contravening her own ethical framework by deciding to break confidentiality or, conversely, will be contravening it, by not breaking confidentiality. She could to some extent avoid this by anonymously revealing the name of the abuser. Although there are occasions when this appears to be the only possible solution, difficulties remain: it reinforces and reflects much of the nature of abuse; it avoids the issue; it is secretive and not completely honest, and it will still impact on the therapeutic relationship. More pragmatically, in this instance the client herself may need to provide information that the counsellor does not have if an investigation is to be effectively undertaken.

Although every counsellor would prefer never to be in this position, it is one that is not uncommon. It is a stark reminder that counselling is not always simply a one-to-one confidential relationship, and that other, larger concerns and moral issues may intrude. Where the well-being and safety of children is involved, confidentiality has to be challenged as an absolute principle. The physical and emotional vulnerability of children provides a strong moral argument for breaking confidentiality, which has clear legal backing. As Jenkins notes: 'According to Lord Justice Eveleigh, "there is no law of confidentiality which could command silence when the welfare of the child is concerned"' (Jenkins, 1997: 132). Such decisions are unpleasant, worrying and stressful but they sometimes cannot be avoided. If confidentiality is broken the counsellor needs to be sure that she has thought carefully about this; has taken it to supervision and has sought advice from those with expertise in the field, including professional associations. As far as is possible, honesty should be maintained throughout with the client, although again there may be exceptional circumstances where this may not be appropriate. It is crucial that throughout the process the counsellor remains both containing and open, helps the client to explore what she is experiencing and feeling, and works with all aspects of the situation, particularly those that are difficult and negative.

CHAPTER 6

Service provision and supervision

6.1 I work in a general practice where I can only occasionally undertake work beyond eight sessions. I know I can refer on some clients for long-term therapy, but there is a long waiting list for such help. What can I achieve in short-term therapy when working with clients who have been abused?

Inevitably the pressure on services to get people through quickly rebounds on abuse survivors. Generally speaking there is not a good match between a survivor struggling to seek help for the first time and short-term or time-limited work, particularly where this is for only six to eight sessions. The criteria for selection for a short-term approach have been listed by a number of therapists (e.g. Malan, 1976, 1979; Molnos, 1995), and although there are variations, one major and basic consideration is whether short-term intervention is likely to increase suffering. Commonly excluded from brief work are those with a history of acting out suicidally, or with addictions or personality disorders, although an exception is found in Ryle (1990, 1997), who describes the successful use of cognitive analytic therapy (usually 16 sessions) with very disturbed patients.

Although opinions vary regarding who is suitable for short-term help, it is generally agreed that clients need to be able to engage quickly with the counsellor and with the process; need to be committed to it, to be sufficiently resilient and well enough supported, and for there to be a clearly defined focus that can be negotiated and agreed as the area to work on. This approach therefore requires the active participation of both parties, and ability in the client to quickly trust the counsellor and the process. Interestingly, how short-term is defined also varies, ranging from precisely three sessions (Barkham and Hobson, 1989) to a less specific number somewhere between four and 50 sessions (Malan, 1976).

The model often used in primary care is referred to in this question, and this setting is inevitably the first port of call for many seeking help. As the literature cited above indicates, the time-limited model can be exceedingly effective for many people, and it has the advantage that it enables people to be seen quickly after the point of referral (Brench and Agulnik, 1998). However, it is often experienced by abuse survivors as invasive, distressing and disturbing: it resonates too strongly with the experience of abuse – it comes at them too fast, in a way that feels hard to control, and where it may be impossible to say no. Although abuse survivors may apparently consent, this may reflect their difficulty in responding any differently since saying no is either dangerous (as it often was in the abuse), or simply not in their emotional vocabulary. Not complying with professionals, especially when a client needs help and feels distressed and worried, requires a high degree of self-confidence and self-belief that is often not the case with abuse survivors. So this approach may stir up issues rather than resolve them, and not allow sufficient time for trust to be built up, tried and tested. This is further exacerbated for the many survivors who have experienced previous professional intervention as abusive or invasive.

In short-term work the process does not easily go at the client's pace, since a clear focus and speed is of the essence. It is particularly problematic when the practitioner is not highly trained and experienced, and therefore may not see the pitfalls. A survivor once described it as like someone taking a big spoon, and stirring up a boiling pot and then leaving her with the resulting mess as it all spilt over. Practitioners who are working in this setting need to exercise considerable care and responsibility if short-term work with abuse survivors is to serve a useful purpose, and not at worst to be abusive. Too often, short-term work is used not because it is appropriate for the client's presentation and need, based on careful assessment, but because it is all that can be offered. Short-term work becomes an imposition, rather than one model to be used amongst others. Abuse survivors have a history of being imposed upon and the counsellor needs to be continually informed by that knowledge.

If short-term work is the only option, this has to be clearly communicated to the client, and then held in mind and actively acknowledged as the sessions progress. Abuse survivors refer, or are referred, at different points in their own journey, and the appropriateness of short-term work is partly dependent on the point they have reached. For some survivors, 'bite-sized' pieces of counselling work well such as the client who has previously received help and is coming with a specific issue they wish to work on. In this instance, if the counsellor stays in tune with the client and responds to what she is bringing there is a clear focus, so that time-limited work can be validating and empowering: the client is heard and her needs responded to. The counsellor, however, has to take care to stay within that agreed focus: counsellors can have their own agendas too, one of which is the belief that the abuse itself must be talked about for recovery to take place; but this may be inappropriate. If the client is presenting with an immediate and defined crisis, responding quickly to that specific situation can be enormously helpful. It is also a very good experience for the survivor that a crisis is taken seriously and a prompt response is given.

The situation is much more complex for survivors needing help for the first time and who do not present with an obvious crisis or a clear issue they wish to work upon. They may be extremely distressed and have no clear idea as to how to progress, and little understanding of the counselling process. To complicate matters further they may not present as abuse survivors. Even identifying themselves as such can be a tortuous and painful acknowledgement, and it may take longer than the six or eight weeks offered to trust the counsellor sufficiently to be able to begin to explore this area. Here the counsellor who suspects abuse must take great care: with a time limit hovering and weeks passing by, it may be tempting to force the pace and impose interventions that are not in fact appropriate. In these instances it is far better to offer the experience of being heard, of being with someone who responds respectfully, carefully and considerately; of having neither themselves nor their experience labelled, but instead having their feelings validated without having to go into the detail of the cause of distress; of not feeling forced into painful revelation or exploration; and of having boundaries acknowledged and held.

This description is perhaps the antithesis of the philosophy of short-term work, in that it does not suggest a specific focus or goal, and simply aims to provide a good experience of being with another person, where there is no exploitation and no misuse of the power dynamic. Such an approach is in itself nurturing, containing and reassuring and can pave the way for further help. Sometimes it can usefully include helping the client to find small ways currently to make life a little easier, but this is not always possible. Acknowledging with the client the limitations of what has been offered whilst also recognizing its value, provides a different model of relating. By offering clarity and openness, combined with respect and solid boundaries, in the context of a non-demanding and non-invasive relationship, the potential and hope for a different way of being is demonstrated.

A limited number of sessions can also provide the opportunity to explore with the client what their longer-term needs may be, while honestly recognizing the waiting time that will be involved in referral. Knowing local resources is essential: many excellent organizations exist that are run by survivors for survivors, and these may either provide sufficient help in themselves, or can be used as an ongoing support until longer-term help is available. These organizations do not suit everyone, especially those who are not ready or do not wish to identify themselves in this way. Assumptions should not be made, but a good knowledge of local resources means the survivor may be able to be linked with the right support or therapy for them.

There is a short-term model of counselling for abuse survivors taking place over six sessions, which Wilson (1993) describes, developed by the Lambeth Women and Children's Health Project. The description is impressive and the model is marked by clarity of thought and planning. It is based on considerable experience and knowledge, and on the basic principle that:

> The project stipulates that women who come for help must take the active step to do so. The woman must make the phone call. When she comes to the project, it is with an explicit awareness that she is coming to work on her feelings and attitudes about her sexual abuse. The project does not treat sexual abuse as an illness. Nor does it foster a dependency on therapy, which can lead some women to feel unable to make a decision without first consulting their therapist. (Wilson 1993: 202)

However, there is a note of caution for those considering this approach. It takes place in a specific project, with considerable expertise, where women referring themselves have already reached a certain stage in their own awareness and readiness. This can be very different to the survivor presenting in primary care.

Another positive description of short-term work with women clients, although not specifically with abuse survivors, is given by Mohamed and Smith (1997), describing their work at the London Women's Therapy Centre. They note that 'we were working with extremely distressed women who might not generally be considered suitable for short term work'. They discuss how short-term work may feel less overwhelming for some women who can be daunted by the prospect of long-term therapy. However, what is evident is that short-term work is offered on the basis of careful assessment, and unlike the counsellor asking this question, in a context where other models are also available, and where in any case short-term work may be as long as 25 weeks.

In discussing the drawbacks to short-term counselling, it must be remembered that open-ended work carries its own risks. The sense of timelessness inherent in approaches which have no specified ending is not always helpful, and can recreate the 'timeless' quality of the abuse, where the child has no idea when it will stop or how long it will go on. In that way, time-limited work can provide a safer boundary, and those working in contexts where they have more choice than the counsellor who asks this question would do well to consider this: longer-term work may be more helpful if an ending is decided at the beginning. For those who do not have the choice, and who can offer only a few sessions, care must obviously be taken not to be abusive, yet it is also important to recognize that the time can be used positively and helpfully, albeit needing very careful management and thought.

Another aspect to consider is this: if working in a time-limited setting where the professional assessment is that this model does not match the needs of a particular client group, this needs to be fed back assertively to those who manage the service and hold the purse strings. Counsellors need to feel sufficient self-confidence and self-belief to ensure that their own voices are heard.

* * *

6.2 I am seriously thinking of starting a group for abuse survivors. What do I need to bear in mind in setting it up?

Perhaps the first point is whether this questioner has a colleague to undertake this work with her. Most practitioners who run groups for survivors would strongly advocate the need for two facilitators (Blake-White and Kline, 1985; Bergart, 1986). Running a group for abuse survivors is demanding and tiring. The support of a colleague is essential, in terms of organizing, taking responsibility for the group and in having someone to share the experience with. It also has considerable benefit to the group members, who may find it easier to relate to one or the other facilitator, although it must be recognized that there is always the risk in groups of one being labelled the 'good' leader, and the other the 'bad'; yet such splitting can be usefully worked with once recognized.

Once the group is under way two key tasks of a group – working with process and working with content – are most smoothly incorporated by two facilitators. It is a major job for one person, especially when the content of the material is often disturbing and distressing. More pragmatically, if one facilitator is unwell or unexpectedly absent, it allows the group to continue with the other still present. It is generally not a good idea for a group that is normally facilitated to carry on alone, especially in its early stages. Both facilitators need to have a good and sound knowledge base of child abuse, of the impact of abuse on the adult, and clearly of the dynamics of groups.

Having found a co-facilitator, another key task is to find a supervisor whom both trust and who similarly has the necessary expertise in groups and abuse. The nature of working with abuse is that it has a profound impact on the counsellor (see Question 5.2) and this is likely to be considerably intensified by the group experience. Transferences and countertransferences are powerful and there needs to be sufficient supervisory time with a skilled supervisor, who can work at this level. Ideally supervision should be of the same frequency as the group, so a group that is meeting weekly is supervised weekly. In addition to formal supervision, the facilitators need some time before the group to establish contact with one another, and further time after the group to debrief the experience, sharing any anxieties about the group itself or about individual members, and any difficult feelings experienced by the facilitators, including towards one another.

Selecting members for the group is a time-consuming but crucial task. Members should want to be in a group, so assessors need to be aware of any external pressure coming from other professionals or from friends or family for the client to attend. It is often felt to be a contraindication for group entry if the client is 'acting out' (for example, self-harming), but as shown in Question 3.6, many survivors self-harm, and if they were all considered inappropriate and excluded, most of the survivors' groups I have known would never have run. Perhaps what is important is whether the client can tolerate exploration and acknowledgement of such acting-out, and feels able in time to share their experience and feelings with others. Many who self-harm have a very clear sense that it is a response, albeit at the moment not controllable, to distress and internal pain, and that recognition in itself is a positive step. However, the inclusion of suicidal clients, as opposed to those who self-harm (which can indeed protect against suicide), needs to be taken very seriously. Being in a group may intensify suicidal feelings, and the other group members may not be able to tolerate this. Those who cannot yet bear to think about or talk about their experiences except in very small doses may be overwhelmed in a group – it can be too much to hear others exploring what they cannot yet safely acknowledge. Clients with drug or alcohol dependency may not be suitable. This partly depends on the skills and knowledge of the facilitators, on the level of substance dependency, and on whether such clients themselves feel they can guarantee to attend in a sober state. If they cannot they will not benefit from the group, and may anger or distress others inappropriately. Some survivors cannot yet tolerate attention being given to others and need to have a person to themselves in order to feel safe and nurtured, and this presentation does not match well with being in a group. Clients who are obviously psychotic should be excluded. Care should be taken before accepting anyone who is severely dissociated, as they are unlikely to benefit. Finally, those who are consistently angrily destructive of others can be difficult to contain safely within a group.

There are many positive indications that someone will benefit from a group, either where a survivor has had no previous help, where a group is seen a positive choice, or where someone has had previous individual help and sees being in a group as a further step forward. The first is a real desire to be with others who have had a similar experience, and a belief that sharing this will be helpful and supportive. Some ability to relate to and to be in contact with others is essential. Groups best suit those who are able to and like to give as well as receive, and believe that their experiences could be useful to someone else. It is important that the survivor can manage without always being the focus of attention. For many survivors this is actively helpful: being the focus of attention as a child has very negative connotations. It is also worth exploring with prospective clients if they feel they will be able to express any anxieties they may feel about the group in the group, rather than internalize them.

When assessing a survivor for suitability for entry to a group it is important that this is experienced as a mutual process. The survivor needs to be encouraged to ask as many questions as she needs to, to share and express any anxieties, to find out fully about the group and to check out the qualifications and experience of the facilitators. The assessor must equally be clear about the group, its duration, purpose and aims, so that the survivor can make an informed choice. It is important that the assessor acquires the necessary information from the survivor, in order to ascertain if the group will be the best option for her. However, great care, as ever, must be taken to ensure that this process is not invasive and does not misuse power: that would be a very poor start. So although some practitioners use questionnaires to elicit information, I do not recommend their use (see Question 1.3). In my experience skilled counsellors can find out what is needed by carefully working with the client in a mutually negotiated exploratory style.

On starting the group, an initial task of the facilitators is to be very clear regarding its ground rules: the time, duration, purpose of the group, attendance, confidentiality, boundaries, and contact outside of sessions (between group members and between group members and facilitators). Other ground rules relate to expectations on group members and safety: for instance, members need to know that noone will force them to speak, that violent and aggressive behaviour is not acceptable, and that they must not be under the influence of drink or drugs when they attend. Facilitators need to be very clear in regard to child protection issues. As the group begins, the facilitators must ensure both the establishment and maintenance of safety and trust, that everyone is heard and has a voice, that noone is lost in the group or becomes a scapegoat. Being 'good enough' parents can be modelled, which includes the facilitators keeping the group to task and ensuring that it becomes a containing, predictable and boundaried space.

Although running a survivors' group is a complex and demanding task, the rewards are great. If carefully set up it can provide an arena where survivors in the company of others can begin to break down barriers of secrecy, learn to trust, come to value their own selves and their capacity to give as well as receive, and move forward in a way that is impressive to observe. Facilitators do, however, need to recognize that although groups can be seen as an economic use of resources, they still need considerable investment of time and energy, both to initiate them and then to run them safely.

* * *

6.3 What are the advantages of self-help groups for survivors and what has to be taken into account when setting them up? Can counsellors have a role in supporting them?

Self-help groups have obvious advantages: those who form them are highly motivated and very committed; members have a shared experience and come together because of it; such groups can be deeply empowering, and can also act as a voice and a pressure group for change. They can develop from facilitated groups (see Question 6.2), especially from time-limited groups where members decide they want more and decide to set up a group for themselves; but many arise simply from the experience of many survivors of not having been helped or heard. Additionally, such groups cost virtually nothing, and as they operate outside the formal structures of care and health services they can reach out to survivors who have been re-victimized within those services, or feel they have failed to meet their needs.

There are some disadvantages. They may have little or no funding and therefore rely on an enormous amount of energy from individual survivors. There need to be enough committed people to form the initial group and to ensure its maintenance. If there are members with serious suicidal feelings, or serious addictions, or who have children currently at risk, this may be too much for the group to contain. It is also problematic if a group member is regularly so distressed and unable to contain this, that they take so much space and time that it is unavailable to others. This can effectively wreck a self-help group: in setting it up initially those involved need to consider if referral routes are available if this occurs.

It is important to check if potential members really want to be in a self-help group and are ready for it: that is, is it what they want or is it all there is? Another aspect to consider is whether there will be an external consultant or supervisor to the group, which is valuable particularly if it does run into difficulty. Other areas to be considered are the same as in setting up any group: for instance, is it to be a closed group, or does it allow new members? Does it allow entry only at a certain point in time, and how and by whom is this to be decided? Another question is how survivors are to make contact. Is there to be a group member who is the initial contact point, who will give out information, and then be responsible for liaising with the group? Self-help groups often have difficulties in finding appropriate accommodation which is reasonably sound-proofed, confidential, consistently available, comfortable and warm. A safe environment is needed and a member's house is often not a good idea, because in the long term this places too much responsibility on one person.

Self-help groups need to decide on the following: a regular time and place to meet; the length of time the group meets for, with a definite ending time – for example, there could be an hour and a half for the group to work, plus half an hour wind-down time for refreshments and general chit-chat. The half hour at the end provides time to move away from issues discussed in the group and move back into everyday life. The frequency of the group needs to be decided: whether it is to be weekly, fortnightly or monthly. The length of time the group meets may partly depend on this frequency. Some self-help groups have a rotating organizer responsible for arranging the venue, informing people of any changes, and ensuring refreshments are available if wanted. This person is not responsible for running the group itself but simply for the practical arrangements. This needs to rotate at agreed intervals, so that it is not too arduous a task.

Some self-help groups use the model of a group being led by a different member each time. This person takes responsibility for starting and finishing on time, ensuring people are heard and that no one individual takes over the group. If this model is used it must be a different member each time and it is helpful to decide a clear rota in advance. Many self-help groups recognize that a key part of their value is members meeting other people who offer support not just during the group but in the time between meetings. If members have access to one another between groups for support it is important to decide whether this is just going to happen informally, or whether there is an explicit and open agreement that this can take place.

There are some difficulties commonly encountered by self-help groups. One relates to the size of the group, that it is either too large or too small. A limit on numbers prevents it becoming unmanageably large. As the group nears this number consideration can be given to forming a second. If numbers are declining and members are being lost the group needs to explore what is causing this and what can be done about it. This can be linked to another common difficulty, that when a few members dominate the group others do not feel heard and as a result leave. If this does occur it needs tackling, since power issues are coming into play just as they did in the various abuse situations the members experienced. The group leaders have to look out for this. Groups can get stuck in one feeling, or in one area of concern, and again this needs to be recognized if the group is to be enabled to move on. It is also highly problematic if issues come up that are so difficult that the group feels out of its depth: this is where availability of external help can be extremely valuable. Some group members may want to deal with aspects of their abuse that other group members cannot yet cope with, and it is important that this can be discussed and a strategy decided on. Once they are aware of these potential pitfalls, group members can often deal with such difficulties when they arise.

The level of involvement and commitment is the core strength of self-help groups, but inevitably it can lead to problems too. Self-help groups can be very powerful and empowering, but they also have their own conflicts and difficulties. A counsellor or therapist who is interested in self-help groups for abuse survivors can therefore occupy a helpful role, if they are accepted by the group, as an external adviser. Many of the difficulties frequently encountered are predictable, but survivors do not necessarily foresee them when setting up self-help groups. The benefit of having someone who is 'outside' the group, as with supervision, is that it provides a more objective perspective that is less visible to those actively involved in the process. Self-help groups often reach the survivors that noone else can. To help them in identifying, acknowledging, and resolving some of the potential or actual pitfalls can be a considerable benefit in assisting them to establish and maintain a very important resource for survivors.

* * *

6.4 I help to run a voluntary agency for abuse survivors. Inevitably the work is very demanding and stressful. I am anxious that the agency itself is supportive and caring to its workers but I know from experience elsewhere that the dynamics of abuse can be recreated in the agency. Workers can feel persecuted both from within the agency and from outside. How can this be understood and dealt with?

This important question contains a number of significant elements. First, there is the nature of voluntary organizations, often struggling with insufficient funding and uncertain futures. They are usually staffed by a combination of volunteers and one or more salaried staff. The staff share a strong commitment but often lack sufficient support (for example, finance and the provision of suitable accommodation), and they often work very hard in a context where they have to contain very distressed clients. The combination of some paid workers and some who are not can be the very strength of such agencies, but can also produce tensions and conflicts.

Second, if it is an agency that deals specifically with survivors of abuse, this inevitably means that powerful feelings and disturbing material will be in abundance, seeping into everyone and affecting everything involved, including the wider organization. Third, voluntary agencies are prone to the same organizational dynamics and tensions as any other organization. These can be powerful and disruptive even in agencies that are more firmly established financially, better supported in other ways and are not dealing with highly distressed people. I have drawn attention in many of these answers to the boundaries that have been attacked in the victim of abuse. There are different issues about boundaries in many voluntary organizations: shortage of resources leads to multi-tasking, which may be inevitable but is not always helpful, since it increases the possibilities of splitting, denial and boundary mismanagement.

It is not therefore surprising that abuse agencies can encounter difficulties. A good starting point in exploring them is to acknowledge the complexity of the task, whilst also recognizing that voluntary organizations have a crucial role in helping abuse survivors. Given the potential pitfalls, it is remarkable that so many remain buoyant, robust and effective. Their work has immeasurable value, and taking pride in it and validating its significance is crucial to the morale of all concerned.

I have addressed in other answers the potential power that abuse has to affect whoever it touches, by triggering difficult and seemingly dangerous feelings. In the original abuse, perpetrators were skilled strategists. They effectively and absolutely denied their responsibility; they projected their difficulties, their violence and their issues into and on to others; they created splits and enforced secrecy. The resulting impact on their victims in terms of trauma and terror inevitably also affects their counsellors and in turn impacts on organizations. Countertransference, and its potential for damage if unrecognized, is discussed in Questions 5.2. and 5.3, and another key concept is that of projective identification:

> This term refers to an unconscious inter-personal interaction in which the recipients of a projection react to it in such a way that their own feelings are affected: they unconsciously identify with the projected feelings ... projective identification frequently leads to the recipients acting out the counter-transference deriving from the projected feelings. (Halton 1994: 16)

Counsellors working in an agency can act out such feelings against it: for example, the counsellor may say that she feels attacked, unsupported, that noone understands, that the agency is too concerned with money and not enough with clients, and that the management is poor. These feelings may be directed generally as an attack against the whole agency, or can be aimed at a particular person seen as having some authority. If this dynamic is not contained, understood and worked with, there is a danger of further contamination, and the agency may act back in a retaliatory or punitive way. The reverse can also happen: those in a managerial capacity, or those who have organizational responsibilities, can also unconsciously act out, directing this at the counsellors. They feel the counsellors do not understand the management's difficulties, that they are not following procedures, they do not understand that they have to conform to agency requirements. Stalemate can result where discussion, negotiation and exploration becomes impossible. The dynamic is very powerful: everyone is convinced it is not their fault, and not their responsibility, and that the other has invited the criticism by their behaviour – which is just how the abuser rationalized the abuse and denied any blame.

This situation is further complicated where managers and organizers also have a practitioner role: the potential for being entangled in splits and projections intensifies and is magnified by the various roles, and the possible conflicts between them. To add to this, the intensity can be further heightened if the workers concerned have a personal interest in, or a history relevant to the survivors the service works with. For instance, a counsellor who previously worked with looked-after children, and was responsible for their well-being, and who now sees survivors of abuse in care, can be particularly vulnerable to feelings of guilt, shame and responsibility. She holds the secret of her previous experiences, and whilst this may not be consciously communicated to the client (indeed is more likely to be consciously withheld) unconscious communication has its own impact. Similarly, agencies are vulnerable where they are set up with a particular brief, or within a particular context, where the workers share common beliefs or experiences with the clients. For example, agencies set up within a specific religious or cultural context, where both clients and workers have the same background, need to exercise great care. If this is not transparent but kept hidden (especially if the workers feel anxiety, guilt or worry that such knowledge would adversely affect their client) the secrecy, lies and deceit of abuse are available for unconscious projection and acting out. The ramifications and possibilities of becoming entangled with powerful, complex unconscious dynamics is huge, and increases relative to these extra complicating factors.

Added to these factors of countertransference and projective identification is another powerful feature, that of work-related anxieties. Obholzer, writing about organizations generally, notes:

> It is important to understand the nature of the anxieties that are stirred up, as well as those inherent in the regular work of the organization. These are,

as we see it, three layers of anxiety that need to be understood before they are addressed: primitive anxieties, anxieties arising out of the nature of the work, and personal anxieties. (1994: 206)

Obholzer defines primitive anxiety as 'the ever present, all pervasive anxiety that besets the whole of human kind'. Anxiety that arises from work is self-explanatory, although it has obvious potency when considering work with abuse survivors.

Personal anxiety similarly has a special resonance in the context of abuse: since it is profoundly anxiety-provoking on a personal level. Menzies (1959) explores the effects of different forms of anxiety in the context of nursing. She examines how the difficult and frightening work of nurses leads to the formation of unconscious defences which then affect all relationships and functioning. As a further tightening of the knot, more defences then form, and difficulties, tensions and anxieties increase. Menzies describes the effect of these dynamics on patient care, and it is evident that if unchecked and unchallenged they lead to less effective care and less motivated workers, who are increasingly unable to cope with decision-making or change.

Clearly, anyone involved in running services for survivors needs to be very aware of the dangers of destructive dynamics becoming embedded in the organization. They lead to unhappy and demoralized staff, who cannot then provide a safe and effective service to their clients. Counsellors may leave; others may feel unsafe; anxiety may abound. The power of abuse to destroy and damage has been allowed to take a further toll. Clients need to know that whatever happens in their work with counsellors can be safely contained. For the counsellor to be able to work effectively she in turn needs to feel held by the agency. For this to happen, all the staff need to have a good awareness and understanding of the difficulties that can arise and of their origins. Openness to discussing difficulties is crucial, so the organization needs a structure, philosophy and culture that facilitates and encourages such discussion and really believes in its value. Staff must be prepared to struggle with difficult and uncomfortable issues, and to go on struggling in an organizational culture that neither blames not shames.

This demands real maturity from workers, combined with a passionate belief in the value of the work. But passion also needs monitoring: if, as suggested above, the worker is too close to the issue or too defensive about certain aspects of it, passion blinds to the reality of what may be occurring. The ability to stand back, observe, think, appraise and take appropriate responsibility is as important as passion. Recognizing negatives, as well as understanding and placing them in the right context, is essential. As they do not go away for the clients so they do not go away for agencies and counsellors either.

Recognizing that trauma is contagious is central to this process: the power of abuse and its potential for destructiveness is considerable and does not stop with individual counsellors. Organizations need help and support too, and need to have resources to contain them in the same way that supervision, training, friends and other interests contain, care for and support the individual counsellor. The organization is even more complex than the individual, so it is vital to address this level of operation and its functioning. In my experience it is this level that is given less consideration and attention, and yet becomes the weak link if it is ignored, so that much avoidable damage and hurt can result. Inbuilt and knowledgeable supervisory support and consultation at an organizational level is essential if the organization itself is to hold and contain effectively the many layers of complex dynamics that inevitably exist, and if it is not to become like an unpredictable pendulum that reacts to every knock to its dynamics.

Other measures also help. Commitment to the work must be demonstrated actively through the provision of adequate support, training and supervision. Reliable, regular and trusted supervision is essential, preferably with supervisors who understand how the effects of abuse impact on the organization. Encouraging counsellors to have other interests and other people in their lives is vital: enjoyment without guilt is important. Clinical involvement in very demanding work needs to be balanced by involvement in other worlds. Counsellors and therapists need to allow themselves to leave their work behind, and agencies can develop a culture that both encourages and models this.

* * *

6.5 It is difficult in the area where I live to find a supervisor who has experience of working with abuse survivors. I wonder whether that means I should limit the work I do with these problems, or would occasional consultancy with an experienced supervisor elsewhere be good practice?

Whenever counselling work is undertaken it is important to ensure both that supervision is adequate and sufficient, and that the counsellor is not overloaded by more work than is manageable. This is particularly pertinent when working with abuse survivors because of the nature of the material and the potential emotional overload on the counsellor. Although there are now more supervisors and counsellors who have specific training in abuse, it remains true that it is an area that is still surprisingly neglected in many training courses. Some supervisors might argue that if they are skilled and trained in supervision that this is sufficient; that specific knowledge is not necessary, and that their skill lies in understanding and working with the supervisory process itself. Whilst that is necessary and important, in my experience of being a supervisor of abuse work and being supervised in it, this is not generally the perception of counsellors and therapists in the field. They want and need a supervisor with knowledge and expertise both of supervision and of abuse; they do not want to spend precious supervisory time explaining the context, and they want their supervisor to be up to date, knowledgeable and aware of the complexities of work with survivors. They do not see their role as educating their supervisor: they expect them to be responsible for their own learning.

For those counsellors in the position of this questioner, who do not easily have suitable expertise available, their dilemma is not irresolvable, though it requires a flexible, fluid and creative consideration of, and response to, supervisory needs. As a first step, anyone in supervision who feels it is not sufficiently meeting their needs should discuss this with their supervisor. Supervisors cannot be skilful in everything, and they need to acknowledge this honestly and explore the issue with supervisees in relation to their particular work. This is an obvious part of the initial contracting, but since needs and workloads change and develop, the supervisory match therefore needs to be an ongoing consideration.

One solution is that suggested in the question. Specialist supervision to work on a particular aspect or with a particular client can be helpful and appropriate. Although this too can be hard to find in some areas, telephone supervision is a possibility, as are occasional face-to-face sessions, which may need to be of a longer duration if travel is involved. I have both used and provided this, and suggested it to supervisees on occasions, and they have found it to be a valuable and skilled resource to draw on. The boundaries need to be clear, in terms of what is taken to regular supervision, and what to the specialist. This is not dissimilar to the position many have experienced in training that involves having more than one supervisor, where all concerned need to be very clear regarding their roles and responsibilities, and the procedures to be followed in case of difficulty.

It is also important for supervisors themselves to be able to refer to others who have specialist knowledge to assist them in their work and role. Everyone needs to recognize that in very complex work other expertise may need to be called on and that this is a mature, sensible and professional decision. It does not represent failure or inadequacy. Although I am not familiar with supervision via e-mail, this is another possibility for those at a distance from a suitable specialist.

My own experience of providing this type of extra supervision is that it has most frequently been requested by those working with dissociative clients and those who have multiple personalities (see Questions 3.3 and 3.4). Given that multiple personality remains a contentious area and many otherwise skilled practitioners have little knowledge of it, or may indeed be dubious about its existence, seeking assistance from someone with particular experience is an ethical and responsible decision. It is particularly complex and confusing work and, because survivors who present in this way are likely to have suffered extreme trauma, it is vital that enormous care is taken to respond appropriately and carefully. Similarly, survivors of ritual abuse, or where an abuse ring has been involved, present extreme difficulties and the provision of good supervision is essential to contain the counsellor who is in the midst of very uncontained and enormously distressing material.

There are other possibilities that may help the counsellor. Finding other practitioners in the area also working with abuse survivors, and setting up a peer support group is immensely helpful and deeply beneficial. It enables the sharing of ideas and experiences; it eases the isolation of working with trauma; and it provides a space in which to reflect honestly and own the feelings aroused by this work. Working with abuse requires more than supervision, and a wider support network is essential, not an optional extra: 'The role of a professional support system is not simply to focus on the tasks of treatment but also to remind the therapist of her own realistic limits and to insist she take as good care of herself as she does of others' (Herman 1992: 153). The other role of a support group can be to explore training needs. Whilst it can be difficult for a lone practitioner to set up training sessions, a group can organize this more easily. Having identified common areas and needs, a possibility is to bring the specialist into the group rather than individuals seeking out the specialist. Groups also have the advantage of using shared knowledge and skills to act as a pressure group for better provision for survivors; members of such a group can identify service gaps and jointly have a more powerful voice than when speaking as individuals. In this way, both the needs of the counsellors and those of their survivor clients may ultimately be better met, whilst at the same time the isolation of working with abuse is eased.

* * *

6.6 I have just started to supervise counsellors in a local counselling centre. Do I have to bear anything particular in mind when supervising both the counsellors, and through them the work with their clients, where they are working with survivors?

When supervising in this context, a good starting point is remembering that abuse in childhood has the potential to inflict deep developmental and intra-psychic damage and that the resulting dynamics can be played out and repeated in the therapeutic relationship in complex and many-layered ways. They can also extend into the supervisory process. As demonstrated in Questions 5.2. and 5.3, counsellors can feel overwhelmed, invaded and haunted by terrible and terrifying scenarios; they can doubt that anything is ever what it seems; and they can feel useless and helpless. Supervisors too can similarly feel overwhelmed and doubt if they have anything helpful to offer, and yet good supervision can provide the safe and secure containment that enables the counsellor to be effective in this very demanding work.

To supervise counsellors working with survivors, clinical experience in the field and a sound and specific knowledge of abuse and its effects is needed. If the supervision is within the context of an agency, experience and knowledge of agencies is needed. As noted in Question 6.4, the dynamics of abuse can spread into organizations, and if not recognized and managed can be destructive. Supervisors, who can be close to the material, the supervisee and the agency, whilst maintaining some distance from them, are in an excellent position to identify such dynamics when those more intimately involved cannot see what is occurring.

Supervisees need to know that their supervisor is resilient and is able to manage the material presented. They need to feel sufficiently safe to unload and to share negative responses and feelings without this being pathologized. However, it is also important to be able to offer constructive challenge and to explore areas of concern. Because the work does not in my view fit neatly into one theoretical model, supervisors are particularly helpful when they have a sound theoretical base yet are also able to work flexibly and creatively in a way that is client led. The supervisor has therefore to offer an experience that is containing but also challenging, whereby the counsellor is helped to identify their feelings and to explore their meaning, whilst also considering the most helpful therapeutic interventions. It is also helpful for the supervisee to learn from their supervisor's knowledge and experience, which can be given without taking over the supervisory space. Finally, given the nature of the work, the supervisor also needs to be watchful of counsellors becoming overloaded, with subsequent unhelpful consequences for either themselves or their clients.

Because abuse attacks trust and safe attachment so deeply and thoroughly this permeates the whole process. As the creation of trust is so basic to the counsellor and client relationship so it is to the supervisory relationship. It must not be persecutory, attacking or critical – if it is, it will not work. Otherwise the supervisee will censor what they say, and what should be an open and honest process is then in danger of becoming a pretence: image with little substance. A relationship has to be created in which the supervisee is able to speak about the most difficult and most perplexing aspects of their work. They need to be able to communicate both the frightening and hidden world of the client and the sometimes frightening and worrying responses they experience. Otherwise there is a danger that the previously unspoken secrets of the client become the unspeakable experience of the counsellor. A key role of supervision is to prevent the isolation of the counsellor mirroring the isolation of the client. Sara Scott (1998: 83) describes how supervision was a 'life-saver' to her when she first worked with a ritual abuse survivor; and this reflects the experience of many when they first encounter such horrors.

In counselling abuse survivors, the projections and transferences can be so powerful and the countertransference so complex and potentially overwhelming (Davies and Frawley, 1994) that it can take away the therapist's ability to think. A significant aspect of supervision is to help the supervisee to recreate a space to think within the supervisory session so that hopefully this then happens within the therapy session too. There is also a particular risk of the countertransference becoming traumatizing for the counsellor (Herman, 1992). If these sometimes highly disturbing experiences and feelings cannot be safely expressed and worked with in supervision they can be acted out dangerously with the client or introjected and harm the counsellor.

If I were to select one aspect of the supervisory process in the context of abuse that is central and essential, it is the need to work with the countertransference. If the supervisee does not trust the supervisor this will not be possible. We know that clients with a history of abuse are particularly vulnerable to being abused by therapists and that female clients are most at risk in a male therapist and female client dyad (Strean, 1993). One way of explaining this (although there are others) is that an erotic countertransference is being acted out. But there are other countertransferential risks. As shown in Question 5.2, there are many variations and patterns all based on overwhelmingly strong feelings which sweep through the person – mirroring the unstoppable and penetrating experience of the abused child.

Trustworthy supervision can actively prevent countertransferential reactions from being dangerously acted out. As a supervisor, it is crucial to be aware of the patterns of countertransference that can evolve, and to have a sound understanding of their origins and psychological and dynamic purpose. Without this it is not possible to work with the supervisee to identify what is happening: a process that involves naming it, creating a safe space for expression of how problematic and disturbing it is to be caught up in something so powerful, and finding safe and therapeutic ways of responding. It is sometimes also crucial to state clearly and firmly when some actions or responses from the therapist are unacceptable. Doing so in a way that is challenging and containing, without becoming destructive or shame inducing, is difficult. But it is possible within the context of a well-established, trusting and respectful relationship.

The recognition of, and the ability to, work with transference and countertransference is a real strength of the psychodynamic approach. But like all strengths it can also be a weakness if misused. Psychodynamic supervisors and therapists acknowledge and work with the real relationship as well as the transferential relationship, and supervisors need to watch that what is reported by the supervisee as transference is not actually an aspect of the real relationship. One example is of a supervisee who reported a negative transference from his client. The client had said that she experienced the therapist as critical and attacking, which the supervisee interpreted as the client experiencing him as her abusive father. But in supervision it became evident that the therapist was in reality being critical and attacking: and this was not the client's transference, but the acting out of the therapist's negative countertransference, which had been quite accurately identified by the client. In denying the reality of his stance, the therapist was in danger of repeating an earlier pattern, in which this client's attempts as a child to tell of her abuse had been explained away as fantasy. Unravelling this type of situation is extremely productive and helpful to counsellors in monitoring their own responses honestly and openly, and in recognizing the power they hold in the relationship. Indeed, the same can apply to supervision: supervisors can be persecutory or patronizing, and this can be reality – and not a consequence of the supervisee's projections.

For practitioners working with abuse survivors, and for the survivors themselves, counselling can be hard, painful work. If the supervisor becomes a safe container for material that feels unmanageable, the counsellor can return to her client less burdened, stronger, more optimistic, more able to think and more secure in herself and her work, with a clearer focus and understanding. The ripple effect of childhood abuse is extraordinarily wide and extensive, but supervision has a crucial role in ensuring that this is made manageable, does not overwhelm, does not become abusive to the counsellor and does not add further distress to an already hurt client.

References

Abel GG, Rouleau JL (1990) The nature and extent of sexual assault. In WL Marshall, DR Laws, HE Barbaree (eds), Handbook of Sexual Assault: Issues, Theories and Treatment of the Offender. New York: Plenum.

Agass D (2000) Containment, supervision and abuse. In U McCluskey, C Hooper (eds), Psychodynamic Perspectives on Abuse: the Cost of Fear. London: Jessica Kingsley Publications.

Aldridge-Morris R (1989) Multiple Personality Disorder. An Exercise in Deception. Hove: Erlbaum.

Allen D M (1980) Young male prostitutes: a psychosocial study. Archives of Sexual Behaviour 9(5): 399–426.

Antony Black J (2000) Multiple personality: a personal perspective. In M Walker, J Antony Black (eds), Hidden Selves: an Exploration of Multiple Personality. Buckingham: Open University Press.

Arnold L, Babiker G (1998) Counselling People Who Self Injure. In Z Bear (ed.), Good Practice in Counselling People who have been Abused. London: Jessica Kingsley Publications.

Bagley C, Young L (1987) Juvenile prostitution and child sexual abuse: a controlled study. Canadian Journal of Community Mental Health 6(1): 5–26.

Barkham M, Hobson F (1989) Exploratory therapy in two-plus-one sessions: a single case study. British Journal of Psychotherapy 6(1): 89–100.

Becker JV, Cunningham-Rathner J, Kaplan MS (1986) Adolescent sexual offenders: Demographics, criminal, and sexual histories, and recommendations for reducing future offences. Journal of Interpersonal Violence 1(4): 431–45.

Bergart AM (1986) Isolation to intimacy: incest survivors in group therapy. Social Casework 266–75.

Bettelheim B (1980) Surviving and Other Essays. New York: Vintage Books.

Blake-White J, Kline CM (1985) Treating the dissociative process in adult victims of childhood incest. Social Casework 394–402.

Bolton FG, Bolton SR (1987) Working with Violent Families: A Guide for Clinical and Legal Practitioners. Beverley Hills, Calif: Sage.

Bolton G, Morris L, MacEachron A (1989) Males at Risk: The Other Side of Child Sexual Abuse. London: Sage.

Bowlby J (1988) A Secure Base. London: Routledge.

Brench J, Agulnik P (1998) The advantages and disadvantages of a brief intervention strategy in a community counselling service. Psychodynamic Counselling 4: 2.

Briere JN (1992) Child Abuse Trauma: Theory and Treatment of the Lasting Effects. Newbury Park, Calif: Sage.

Briere J, Runtz M (1998) Post sexual abuse trauma: data and implications for clinical practice. Journal of Interpersonal Violence 2(4): 367–79.

Briggs D (1998) Men as victims of sexual abuse, men as abusers. In Z Bear (ed.), Good Practice in Counselling People Who have Been Abused. London: Jessica Kingsley Publications.

British Psychological Society (1995) Report on Recovered Memory. Leicester: The British Psychological Society.

Burgess AW, Groth A, McCausland MP (1981) Child sex initiation rings. American Journal of Orthopsychiatry 51: 110–18.

Burstow B (1992) Radical Feminist Therapy. Working in the Context of Violence. Newbury Park, Calif: Sage.

Carnes P (1983) The Sexual Addiction. Minneapolis: CompCare.

Casement P (1994) The wish not to know. In V Sinason (ed.), Treating Survivors of Satanic Abuse. London: Routledge.

Cassidy J (1999) She was young, naïve – anorexic. Then she fell prey to a professor's 'caring' touch. The Observer. 13 June 1999.

Cawson P, Wattam C, Brooker S, Kelly G (2000) Child Maltreatment in the United Kingdom. London: NSPCC Publications.

Davies JM, Frawley MG (1994) Treating the Adult Survivor of Childhood Sexual Abuse: A Psychoanalytic Perspective. New York: Basic Books.

De Zulueta F (1993) From Pain to Violence: The Traumatic Roots of Destructiveness. London: Whurr Publications.

de Young M (1982) The Sexual Victimization of Children. Jefferson, NC: McFarland.

Department of Health (1991) Working Together Under the Children Act 1989. A Guide to Arrangements for Inter-Agency Co-operation for the Protection of Children from Abuse. London: HMSO.

Egeland B (1988) Breaking the cycle of abuse: implications for prediction and intervention. In K Browne, C Davies, P Stratton (eds), Early Prediction and Prevention of Child Abuse. Chichester: John Wiley.

Egeland B, Jacobvitz D, Papatola K (1987) Inter-generational continuity of parental abuse. In J Lancaster, R Gelles (eds), Biosocial Aspects of Child Abuse. New York: Jossey-Bass.

Erikson E (1965) Childhood and Society. Harmondsworth: Penguin.

Fairbairn WRD (1952) An Object Relations Theory of the Personality. New York: Basic Books.

Ferenczi S (1932) Confusion of tongues between adults and the child. In S Ferenczi (1955) Final Contributions to the Problems and Methods of Psychoanalysis. London: Hogarth Press.

Finch S M (1967) Sexual activity of children with other children and adults. Clinical Pediatrics 3: 1–2.

Finkelhor D (1979) Sexually Victimised Children. New York: Free Press.

Finkelhor D (1984a) Child Sexual Abuse: New Theory and Research. New York: Free Press.

Finkelhor D (1984b) Sexual Abuse of Boys. In AW Burgess (ed.), Research Handbook on Rape and Sexual Assault. New York: Garland.

Freud A (1967) Comments on Trauma. In S Furst (ed.), Psychic Trauma. New York: Basic Books.

Freud S (1920) Beyond the Pleasure Principle. London: Penguin Freud Library, Volume 11.

Freud S, Breuer J (1895) Studies on Hysteria. London: Penguin Freud Library, Volume 3.

Freund K, Kuban M (1993) Toward a testable developmental model of pedophilia: the development of erotic age preference. Child Abuse and Neglect 17(2): 315–324.

Fromm E (1991) Causes for the patient's change in analytic treatment, Journal of Contemporary Psychoanalysis 27: 581–601.

Gabbard G (1989) Sexual Exploitation in Professional Relationships. Washington, DC: American Psychiatric Press.

Groth N, Burgess A (1979) Sexual trauma in the life histories of rapists and child molesters. Victimology: an International Journal 4: 10–16.

Hacking I (1995) Rewriting the Soul. Multiple Personality and the Sciences of Memory. Princeton, NJ: Princeton University Press.

Hall L, Lloyd S (1989) Surviving Child Sexual Abuse. Lewes: The Falmer Press.

Halton W (1994) Some unconscious aspects of organizational life: contributions from psychoanalysis. In A Obholzer, VZ Roberts (eds), The Unconscious at work: Individual and Organizational Stress in the Human Services. London: Routledge.

Herman JL (1981) Father–Daughter Incest. Cambridge, Mass: Harvard University Press.

Herman JL (1988) Considering sex offenders: a model of addiction. Signs 13(4): 695–724.

Herman JL (1992) Trauma and Recovery. New York: Basic Books/London: Pandora.

Herman JL, Schatzow E (1987) Recovery and verification of memories of childhood sexual abuse. Psychoanalytic Psychology 4: 1–14.

Hooper C (1995) Women and their children's experience of sexual violence: rethinking the links. Special issue on women in families and households. Women's Studies International Forum 18(3): 349–60.

Hopkins J (1992) Secondary abuse. In A Bannister (ed.), From Hearing to Healing: Working with the Aftermath of Childhood Sexual Abuse. London: Longman/NSPCC.

Hunter RS, Kilstrom N (1979) Breaking the cycle in abusive families. American Journal of Psychiatry 136: 1320–22.

Jacobs JL (1994) Victimized Daughters: Incest and the Development of the Female Self. London: Routledge.

Janet P (1889) L'Automatisme Psychologique. Paris: Baillière.

Jehu D, Gazan M (1983) Psychosocial adjustment of women who were sexually victimised in childhood or adolescence. Canadian Journal of Community Mental Health 2(2): 71–82.

Jehu D, Gazan M, Klassen C (1984) Common therapeutic targets among women who were sexually abused in childhood. Journal of Social Work and Human Sexuality, 3: 25–45.

Jenkins P (1997) Counselling, Psychotherapy and the Law. London: Sage Publications.

Johnson TC (1993) Preliminary findings. In E Gil, T C Johnson (eds), Sexualized Children: Assessment and Treatment of Sexualized Children and Children Who Molest. Rockville, Md: Launch.

Kempe RS, Kempe CH (1978) Child Abuse. London: Fontana.

Kennedy H, Grubin D (1992) Patterns of denial in sex offenders. Psychological Medicine 22: 191–6.

Kleber RJ, Figley CR, Gerson BPR (eds), (1995) Beyond Trauma: Cultural and Societal Dynamics. New York: Plenum Press.

Klein M (1975) Envy and Gratitude and Other Works 1946–1963. London: Hogarth Press and the Institute of Psychoanalysis.

Kluft RP (1990) On the apparent invisibility of incest: a personal reflection on things known and forgotten. In RP Kluft (ed.), Incest Related Symptoms of Adult Psychopathology. Washington, DC: American Psychiatric Press.

Kohut H (1977) The Restoration of Self. New York: International Universities Press.

Langmade C (1988) The impact of pre- and post-pubertal onsetting incest experience in adult women as measured by sex anxiety, sex guilt, sexual satisfaction and sexual behaviour. Dissertation Abstracts International 44: 917b.

McCann IL, Pearlman LA (1990) Vicarious traumatisation: a contextual model for understanding the effects of trauma on helpers. Journal of Traumatic Stress 3: 131–9.

McFayden A, Hanks H, James C (1993) Ritual abuse: a definition. Child Abuse Review 2: 35–41.

Malan DH (1976) The Frontier of Brief Psychotherapy. New York: Plenum.

Malan DH (1979) Individual Psychotherapy and the Science of Psychodynamics. London: Butterworth.

Masson J (1992) Against Therapy. London: Harper Collins.

Matthews C (1986) No Longer a Victim. Canberra: Acorn Press.

Meiselman KC (1978) Incest: a Psychological Study of Causes and Effects with Treatment Recommendations. San Francisco: Jossey-Bass.

Mendel M (1995) The Male Survivor: The Impact of Sexual Abuse. Newbury Park, Calif: Sage.

Menzies IEP (1959) The functioning of social systems as a defence against anxiety: a report on the nursing service of a general hospital. Human Relations 1: 95–121.

Midgely N (2002) Child dissociation and its 'roots' in adulthood. In V Sinason (ed.), Attachment, Trauma and Multiplicity. Hove: Brunner Routledge.

Mohamed C, Smith R (1997) Time limited psychotherapy. In M Lawrence, M Maguire (eds), Psychotherapy with Women: Feminist Perspectives. London: Macmillan.

Mollon P (1994) The impact of evil. In V Sinason (ed.), Treating Survivors of Satanic Abuse. London: Routledge.

Mollon P (1996) Multiple Selves, Multiple Voices. Working With Trauma, Violation and Dissociation. Chichester: Wiley.

Mollon P (1998) Terror in the consulting room. In V Sinason (ed.), Memory in Dispute. London: Karnac Books.

Mollon P (1999) Multiple selves, multiple voices, multiple transferences. In M Walker, J Antony Black (eds), Hidden Selves: an Exploration of Multiple Personality. Buckingham: Open University Press.

Molnos A (1995) A Question of Time. London: Karnac.

Mondimore FM (2000) Sexual orientation and abuse. In U McCluskey, C Hooper (eds), Psychodynamic Perspectives on Abuse: The Cost of Fear. London: Jessica Kingsley Publications.

Moore A (1999) I was seduced by my counsellor. You. 9 May 1999.

Obholzer A (1994) Afterword. In A Obholzer, VZ Roberts (eds), The Unconscious at Work: Individual and Organizational Stress in the Human Services. London: Routledge.

Offshe R, Watters E (1995) Making Monsters. False memory, Psychotherapy and Sexual Hysteria. London: Andre Deutsch.

Oliver J, Taylor A (1971) Five generations of ill-treated children in one family pedigree. British Journal of Psychiatry 119: 473–80.

Oppenheimer R (1985) Adverse sexual experiences in childhood and clinical eating disorders: a preliminary description. Journal of Psychiatric Research 19: 357–61.

Palmer RL, Oppenheimer R, Chaloner DA, Howells K (1990) Childhood sexual experiences with adults reported by women with eating disorders: an extended series. British Journal of Psychiatry 156: 699–703.

Petrovich M, Templer D (1984) Heterosexual molestation of children who later become rapists. Psychological Reports 54: 810.

'Poppy' (2001) The victim's tale: 'Poppy'. In R Casemore (ed.), Surviving Complaints Against Counsellors and Psychotherapists. Ross-on-Wye: PCCS Books.

Prince M (1906/1957) Dissociation of a Personality. New York: Meridian.

Prince M (1914) The Unconscious. New York: Macmillan.

Prince M (1919) The psychogenesis of multiple personality. Journal of Abnormal Psychology 14: 225–80.

Putman FW (1989) Diagnosis and Treatment of Multiple Personality Disorder. New York: Guilford Press.

Reading B, Jacobs M (2003) Addiction: Questions and Answers for Counsellors and Therapists. London: Whurr Publishers.

Reviere S L (1996) Memory of Childhood Trauma. New York: Guilford Press.

Rosenfeld H R (1971) A clinical approach to the psychoanalytic theory of the life and death instincts: an investigation into the aggressive aspects of narcissism. International Journal of Psycho-analysis 52: 169–78.

Ross C (1989) Multiple Personality Disorder: Diagnosis, Clinical Features and Treatment. New York: Wiley.

Russell DEH (1984) Sexual Exploitation: Rape, Child Sexual Abuse and Workplace Harassment. Beverley Hills, Calif: Sage.

Russell D (1986) The Secret Trauma: Incest in the Lives of Girls and Women. New York: Basic Books.

Russell J (1993) Out of Bounds: Sexual Exploitation in Counselling and Therapy. London: Sage.

Rutter P (1990) Sex in the Forbidden Zone. London: Aquarius Press.

Ryle A (1990) Cognitive Analytic Therapy: Active Participation in Change. Chichester: Wiley.

Ryle A (1997) Cognitive Analytic Therapy and Borderline Personality Disorder. Chichester: Wiley.

Salter A (1989) Accuracy of Expert Testimony in Child Sexual Abuse Cases: a Case Study of Ralph Underwager and Holida Wakefield. New England: New England Commissioners of Child Welfare Agencies.

Salter A (1995) Transforming Trauma. London: Sage.

Sargant W (1967) The Unquiet Mind. London: Heinemann.

Schacter L, Norman K, Koutstaal W (1997) The recovered memories debate. In M Conway (ed.), Recovered Memories and False Memories. Oxford: Oxford University Press.

Scharff JS, Scharff DE (1994) Object Relations Therapy of Physical and Sexual Trauma. Northvale, NJ: Jason Aronson.

Scott S (1998) Counselling survivors of ritual abuse. In Z Bear (ed.), Good Practice in Counselling People Who Have Been Abused. London: Jessica Kingsley Publications.

Sgroi SM, Sargent NH (1993) Impact and treatment issues for victims of childhood abuse by female perpetrators. In M Elliott (ed.), Female Sexual abuse of Children: the Ultimate Taboo. London: Longman.

Shengold L (1979) Child abuse and deprivation: soul murder. Journal of the American Psychoanalytic Association 27: 533–53

Simonds SL (1994) Bridging the Silence: Non-verbal Modalities in the Treatment of Adult Survivors of Childhood Sexual Abuse. New York: WW Norton.

Sinason V (1994) Introduction. In V Sinason (ed.), Treating Survivors of Satanic Abuse. London: Routledge.

Soothill KL, Gibbens TCN (1978) Recidivism of sexual offenders: a re-appraisal. British Journal of Criminology 18(3): 267–76.

Spanos N P (1996) Multiple Identities and False Memories. A Sociocognitive Perspective. Washington, DC: American Psychological Association.

Steele BF, Pollock CB (1968) A psychiatric study of parents who abuse infants as small children. In RE Helfer, CH Kempe (eds), The Battered Child. Chicago: Chicago University Press.

Stern D (1985) The Interpersonal World of the Infant. New York: Basic Books.

Strean H S (1993) Therapists Who Have Sex With Their Patients: Treatment and Recovery. New York: Brunner Mazel.

Underwager R (1993) Interview: Holida Wakefield and Ralph Underwager. Paidika – The Journal of Paedophilia 3: 1.

van der Volk BA, Perry J, Herman JL (1991). Childhood origins of self-destructive behaviour. American Journal of Psychiatry 148 (12): 1665–71.

van der Kolk B, van der Hart O, Marmar C (1996) Dissociation and information processing in post-traumatic stress disorder. In B van der Kolk, A McFarlane, L Weisaeth (eds), Traumatic Stress. New York: Guilford.

Vas Dias S (2000) Inner silence: one of the impacts of emotional abuse upon the developing self. In U McCluskey, CA Hooper (eds), Psychodynamic Perspectives on Abuse. London: Jessica Kingsley Publications.

Walker M (1992) Surviving Secrets: the Experience of Abuse for the Child, the Adult and the Helper. Buckingham: Open University Press.

Walker M (1996) Working with abused clients in an institutional setting: holding hope amidst despair. In E Smith (ed.), Integrity and Change: Mental Health in the Marketplace. London: Routledge.

Walker M (1997) Feminist psychotherapy and sexual abuse. In B Seu, C Heenan (eds), Feminism and Psychotherapy. London: Sage.

Walker M (1999) The inter-generational transmission of trauma: the effect of abuse on the survivor's relationship with their children and on the children themselves. European Journal of Psychotherapy, Counselling and Health 2(3): 281–96.

Walker M (2001) Working safely: counsellor competence. In R Casemore (ed.), Surviving Complaints Against Counsellors and Psychotherapists. Ross-on-Wye: PCCS Books.

Walker M, Antony Black J(eds) (1999) Hidden Selves: an Exploration of Multiple Personality. Buckingham: Open University Press.

Warner-Kearney D (1987) The nature of grooming behaviour used by sexual offenders in father–daughter incest. Paper presented at the Western Criminology Association, Las Vegas, Nev.

Webster M (1998) Emotional abuse in therapy. Self and Society 26: 1.

Williams LM (1992) Adult memories of childhood abuse: preliminary findings from a longitudinal study. In special issue on child and adult memory, The Advisor, Journal of the American Professional Society on the Abuse of Children 5(3): 19–20.

Wilson M (1993) Crossing the Boundary: Black Women Survive Incest. London: Virago.

Wolf R (1998) Becoming real. In Z Bear (ed.), Good Practice in Counselling People Who Have Been Abused. London: Jessica Kingsley Publications.

Yates A (1991) Childhood sexuality. In M Lewis (ed.), Child and Adolescent Psychiatry: A Comprehensive Textbook. Baltimore: Williams and Wilkins.

Youngson SC (1993) Ritual abuse: consequences for professionals. Child Abuse Review 2(4).

Index

Shengold L 86, 89
short-term counselling/therapy 69, 115–119
sibling abuse 39, 40
siblings 87
silence 4, 16, 17, 20, 71, 74
Simonds S L 60
Sinason V 83
sleeping difficulties 11
Smith R 118
Social Services 112, 113
social skills 62, 81
Soothill KL 112
soul murder 86, 89
Spanos NP 55
space 45, 105
speaking, difficulty in 19
splitting 7, 48, 51, 63, 87, 92, 125, 126
statutory obligation 112
Steele BF 23
stereotypes 8
Stern D 6
stranger abuse 8
Strean H S 103, 132
substance abuse 10, 40, 41–2, 61, 88, 106, 120, 121, 122
suggestion 55
suicide/suicidal thought and action 8, 14, 62, 87, 89, 106, 115, 120, 122
suitability for counselling 105–7
superego 48
supervision 25, 66, 70, 94, 95, 98, 100, 112, 113, 114, 119, 120, 122, 124, 128–133
survivor led services 117–118

Taylor A 23
Templer D 9
therapeutic
  alliance 55, 57
  interventions 4, 13, 15, 56, 66, 76, 102, 111
  issues 17–18
  relationship 19, 25, 26, 37, 69, 74, 94, 114
therapist abuse 102–5
therapist survivors 91–3
threats 14, 38, 82, 111
time limits 21, 122

timing of interventions 12, 19, 20, 52, 106
toddlers 47
torture 1, 3, 82, 83, 93
touch 58
transference 26, 52, 57, 70, 74, 119, 132–3
transitional, transitions 47, 77
traumatization of practitioners 84
traumatogenic 55
'truth drugs' 107
trust 18–21, 53, 65, 69, 87, 97, 102, 103, 104, 115, 119, 121, 132

unconscious 48, 57, 59, 64, 88, 98, 113, 126, 127
Underwager R 107, 108
unpredictability of abuse 4

van der Hart O 50, 61
van der Volk B A 50, 61
Vas Dias S 4
victimisation 8, 9, 102, 109
violence 1, 4, 5, 6, 45, 84, 106, 109
visualisation 59
voluntary organisations 124–28

Walker M 3, 4, 7, 23, 29, 30, 87, 98, 99, 105
Warner-Kearney D 19
Wattam C 73
Watters E 85
Webster M 103
Williams LM 109
Wilson M 118
witness, witnessing 39
witness guilt 97
Wolf R 71, 72, 103
World War II 48, 109
women survivors 26
working alliance 25
Working Together under the Children Act 112
workloads 99, 132
worst scenarios 36

Yates A 38
young people, working with 77–80
Young L 91
Youngson SC 84